WALKING IN
THE PEAK DISTRICT –
WHITE PEAK EAST

WALKING IN THE PEAK DISTRICT – WHITE PEAK EAST

42 WALKS IN DERBYSHIRE INCLUDING BAKEWELL, MATLOCK AND STONEY MIDDLETON

by Paul Besley

JUNIPER HOUSE, MURLEY MOSS,
OXENHOLME ROAD, KENDAL, CUMBRIA LA9 7RL
www.cicerone.co.uk

© Paul Besley 2020
Third edition 2020
ISBN: 978 1 85284 976 4
Reprinted 2022
Second edition 2009
First edition 2004

Printed in Czechia on responsibly sourced paper on behalf of Latitude Press Ltd

A catalogue record for this book is available from the British Library.
All photographs are by the author unless otherwise stated.

© Crown copyright 2020 OS PU100012932

Additional route mapping by Lovell Johns www.lovelljohns.com
© Crown copyright 2020 OS PU100012932.
NASA relief data courtesy of ESRI

In memory of Daniel Sells

Updates to this guide

While every effort is made by our authors to ensure the accuracy of guidebooks as they go to print, changes can occur during the lifetime of an edition. Any updates that we know of for this guide will be on the Cicerone website (www.cicerone.co.uk/976/updates), so please check before planning your trip. We also advise that you check information about such things as transport, accommodation and shops locally. Even rights of way can be altered over time. We are always grateful for information about any discrepancies between a guidebook and the facts on the ground, sent by email to updates@cicerone.co.uk or by post to Cicerone, Juniper House, Murley Moss, Oxenholme Road, Kendal, LA9 7RL.

Register your book: To sign up to receive free updates, special offers and GPX files where available, register your book at www.cicerone.co.uk.

Front cover: Descending a miners path into Bonsall (Walk 24)

CONTENTS

Acknowledgements

Writing a walking guidebook is always a collaboration between people. While researching the walks in this book I talked with local people who gave me a wealth of information that helped to add interest and depth to my words. There were too many to mention here but I owe them a great deal.

Mark Richards deserves much of the credit for getting me involved in book writing; without his help this book would never have existed. I owe a big thank you to the team at Cicerone Press: Joe Williams, Andrea Grimshaw, Sian Jenkins, Hannah Stevenson, Felicity Laughton, Amy Hodkin and Caroline Draper.

Some people gave more than a few words and accompanied me on the walks, checked the accuracy of the directions and generally kept nudging me forward. I would specifically like to thank Alison Counsell, Gail Ferriman, David Mason – along with Megan and Griff – Tony Hood, Dave Torr and Ian Wood. And a special mention to Scout, my Border collie walking companion. Thank you all for your companionship and advice.

I need to thank Mark Goodwin and Jo Dacombe for allowing me to use Mark's wonderful poem that Jo inscribed into rock on Walk 4. Art and landscape have a long history of friendship and I feel it is important that we celebrate the two in situ whenever we can.

Finally, and most importantly, my family: Alison Counsell, my partner of many years, and our dogs Olly, Monty and Scout. You all made it so enjoyable.

Features on the overview map

.... County/Unitary boundary

Urban area

National Park
eg **PEAK DISTRICT**

Relief

800m
600m
400m
200m
75m
0m

Route symbols on the 1:50,000 OS map extracts (Walks 1–35) and 1:100,000 route maps (Walks 36–42)

~ route (1:50,000 OS maps)

~ route (1:100,000 route maps)

SF start/finish point

S start point

F finish point

> route direction

(for OS legend see printed OS maps)

Additional symbols on the 1:100,000 route maps

station/railway

SCALE: 1:100,000

0 kilometres 1 2

0 miles 1

Contour lines are drawn at 50m intervals and highlighted at 200m intervals.

Relief

700m
600m
500m
400m
300m
200m
100m

GPX files for all routes can be downloaded free at www.cicerone.co.uk/976/GPX.

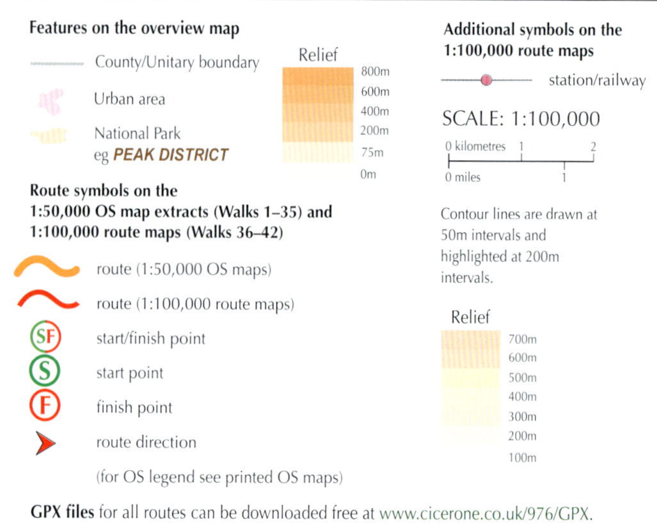

The Sherwood Foresters Monument (Walk 28)

Leawood Pumphouse, High Peak Junction, Cromford (Walk 28)

The Cork Stone, Stanton Moor (Walk 20)

INTRODUCTION

Always take time to rest and enjoy the view (Walk 21)

Walking in the White Peak landscape is a restorative experience. The gentle rolling hills, the long sinewy dales, the green grass and white limestone flecked with the vivid eye-catching primary colours of wildflowers – all fill the mind and body with a sense of wellbeing. Time is the essence of this landscape and it should be spent wisely and slowly in order to capture all it has to offer.

Although formed during the carboniferous period, the human hand is prominent in the White Peak. The green pastures, so essential for the sheep that inhabit much of the countryside, are man-made; their development dependent on the many limekilns that still dot this landscape. The limestone walls that are so evocative of the area tell a story of continuing development of common lands for private use. The green lanes crossing the plateau and dales show how humans moved between the isolated villages and areas of work.

White Peak villages are beautiful. These small isolated communities are

11

little changed even with the arrival of the car. Many have churches that date back to Norman times, often retaining original medieval features. These are wonderful buildings, full of local and national history and are a delight to visit on a hot summer day.

If there is one piece of advice I would give walkers it is to take your time. This is not a landscape of the arduous epic. It is a land of mystery, story and magic. I once led a group of people into a White Peak dale after snow had fallen all night long. As the morning winter sun tried to spread a little warmth, we stood at the entrance to a long, narrow valley. The only sound to be heard was the crystal-clear stream babbling along the floor of the dale. The landscape was covered in a thick blanket of snow as though some magical hand had folded bright white meringue across the dale. A single robin worked its way over the peaks and folds, its red breast vivid against the pure white landscape. All was quiet and, perhaps because of that, we entered the dale in silence, continuing our solitary contemplations as we moved through this real-life Narnia. At the end we emerged onto a road so deep in snow the hedgerow had all but vanished. We never said a word but, as we looked at one another, we knew we had just experienced something personal, something magical, and that it was ours alone to keep. I hope you find your own special corner of this magical landscape.

GEOLOGY

The Peak is formed of a gritstone cap, interspersed with shale, mudstone and coal, that sits above a limestone bed. These two geological features form the two areas commonly known as the Dark Peak and the White Peak. The Dark Peak landscape of gritstone is often joined by peat moor and bog, particularly on the northern and eastern fringes, but outcrops of gritstone do appear as far south as Matlock. Walkers in the White Peak will experience a limestone landscape laid down around 360 million years ago when the area was covered in a tropical sea. The sea creatures that lived and died formed the limestone bed that is almost 2000 metres thick in some areas. Over the millions of years that followed, the White Peak developed two distinct types of landscape: the limestone plateau and the limestone dales.

One of the three main types of limestone found in the Peak District, 'shelf limestone' has the greatest depth in all the area. The rolling landscape of rounded hills and convex slopes running down to rivers at the bottom of the many dales is indicative of this type of geological structure. The second type, 'basin limestone', can be found in the southern area of the Peak. It is much darker in colour and has significantly less depth than shelf limestone. Both shelf and basin limestone are subject to weathering and erosion, which are often seen today in the deep pitting on the surface of the rock. The final type is 'reef limestone', formed from settlement within the tropical ocean. This limestone holds the fossil record of billions of creatures and has escaped much of the erosion seen in the previous types. It is very hard wearing, evidenced by the many reef knolls that populate the southern part of the White Peak, the best example being Thorpe Cloud at the foot of Dovedale. This fossil record of crinoids, known locally as 'Derbyshire screws', can be seen in the walls, stiles and footpaths that have given human shape to this landscape.

Other types of limestone occasionally emerge from the land. Dolomitized limestone gave rise to the oddly placed tor at Harboro Rocks. Volcanic rock, locally called 'toadstone', is often associated with the ancient watercourses. Ashford Black Marble, a very dense, finely grained limestone, is found in only a few quarries around Ashford in the Water. Once worked, it produces highly decorative ornamental pieces.

On the northern and eastern fringes, the gritstone layer is still much in evidence, producing the long 'edges' that sit above the valley floor, then occasionally surfacing as seemingly isolated tors, such as the ones found at Robin Hood's Stride near Harthill, and Black Rock near Cromford.

Looking across 60 million years, gritstone to limestone

The White Peak is rich in mineral deposits of copper, fluorspar, calcite and particularly lead. The minerals sitting in veins that run through the limestone bed to great depths have been mined since well before Roman times. In the 19th century these geological features formed the basis of a huge mining industry in the White Peak. Villages such as Bonsall, Wirksworth and Winster were important mining centres. Today the mining is all but gone, although the towns and villages still retain the buildings and grandeur that resulted from the wealth the industry brought to the communities. It also provided the beautifully walled lanes enjoyed by walkers today that were originally access tracks to and from the mines. Fluorspar is still mined at Glebe Mine in the north of the limestone plateau, the mineral being important in the production of chemicals and metallurgical goods. To see an excellent example of what the mines used to look like, visit the Magpie Mine near Sheldon (Walk 19).

Any visitor to the White Peak will see the giant limestone quarries that abound on the plateau. Although these have only scratched the surface of a 1.2 mile (2km) limestone bed, they are still significant holes in the ground. They cater for our seemingly endless need for road stone, building materials and cement and it is perhaps worth reflecting on how our own needs affect the landscape that we seek to enjoy.

PLANTS AND WILDLIFE

The White Peak is a rich tapestry of interconnecting habitats, from managed pasture, steep limestone slopes and ancient woodland to meadow, watercourse and roadside verge.

This landscape hosts a wide variety of plants and animals, some of which are location dependent and some are important for their rarity. Until the Middle Ages the landscape remained essentially untouched, except in the immediate environs of hamlets and villages. The surrounding land was used for crop production on the feudal ridge and furrow system, whereby each member of the community was responsible for a strip of land and the production of crops for the landowner and fellow villagers. The introduction of sheep onto the land caused a change in its management. Farmers built limekilns and spread the lime onto the surrounding fields to encourage the healthy growth of grass for grazing. Today many of the limekilns survive and offer an important record of the land's use.

Successive Enclosure Acts and the management techniques brought in by the monastic landlords changed the way in which the land was used. But the slopes that bounded the dales were too steep for crops and remain untouched, except for the few sheep that chose to graze there. A diverse collection of plant life thrives on these slopes, including cowslip, wild thyme and early purple orchid, as well as the rare Jacob's ladder.

Wildflowers are abundant in the White Peak

Where sheep cannot gain access, the slopes are covered in rich ferns. Meadows grown for winter feed provided a rich habitat for oxeye daisy, buttercup and knapweed. In the 20th century these meadows fell out of favour and many were destroyed or cultivated for crop growing. Today their significance to local and national wildlife has been noted and meadows are making a comeback in the Peak. A wonderful example of their importance has been the support they have provided the curlew, a bird that has seen a steep decline in recent years.

The Enclosure Acts brought about a fragmented landscape, delineated by limestone walls that often separated livestock from vital water sources. The ingenious solution was the dewpond. These large, circular, man-made ponds, shaped like a dessert bowl, collected and held rainwater to be used by stock. They were an important part of the highly managed farming process. But as sheep farming declined the dewponds fell out of use and into disrepair. Some are being rehabilitated as they provide a perfect habitat for the great crested newt.

Drive along any road in the White Peak and you will see a wonderful display of plant life in the verges. The profusion of colour in spring and early summer, such as the purple meadow cranesbill, is often a good indicator of an old route, especially if accompanied by ancient hawthorn hedgerows.

To the north and east lie the gritstone and peat fringes. Here you will find the wonderful heather, spectacular in August with its vivid pink blooms spreading out across the dark colour of the stone and peat. Hare and grouse abound on the moors along with curlew, ring ouzel and yellow hammer. The common lizard can also be found on the moors and adders are often seen basking in sunlight on footpaths. The adder is our only poisonous snake, so treat it with caution and leave it alone.

In the dales, the rivers are teaming with life. The crystal-clear waters support the wild rainbow trout, wild brown trout and grayling, as well as Britain's own freshwater white-clawed crayfish. Water voles can be found along the banks and dippers skip over the riverbed.

Many of the dales flood during periods of heavy rain, making walking a rather sloshy affair. At times of drought some streams disappear altogether as they seek a route underground within the limestone bed, only to re-emerge many miles further downstream; the River Lathkill is a perfect example of this.

Paths along the streams are often accompanied by woodland and it is not unusual to be surrounded in late spring or early summer by bluebells or the heady aroma of wild garlic while you walk.

As always, nature should be observed and never removed from its own habitat. In several cases removal of a plant or wildlife from its habitat is a criminal offence and should be avoided at all cost.

HISTORY

The first confirmed sign of human activity in the White Peak dates back to the Mesolithic period. Flint shards found around Kniveton, Parwich and above Monsal Dale indicate that settlements of sorts were being established in the area. It was between the Neolithic period and the Bronze Age that permanent settlements were established, mostly in the southern part of the Peak District.

Look at the Ordnance Survey OL24 map of the White Peak and note the number of hills that are accompanied by the word 'Tumulus', denoting an ancient burial site. The more prominent, both in the landscape and standing within these ancient communities, are situated on a 'low', from the Old English word *hlaw* meaning mound or barrow. Minninglow, high up on the limestone plateau, dates from between 3400 and 2400BC and contains two barrows and a chambered tomb. Its position indicates that the residents were of significant standing. Perhaps the best-known 'low' is Arbor Low, situated near today's A515, which has itself been a major route for many centuries. Arbor Low is one of the country's most important ancient monuments and was one of the first to gain scheduled monument status in Britain. Today, small monoliths bearing the letters VR and GR (for Victoria Regina and Georgius Rex) positioned near the entrances to the henge signify continued protection. This Neolithic henge is linked to an

Arbor Low Neolithic henge (Walk 23)

earlier barrow on Gib Hill, some 300 metres away.

Evidence of Bronze Age activity abounds across the Peak. Stone circles along with cairn fields, hut circles and rock art of cup and ring circles dot the land. Stanton Moor has a wealth of sites, the most famous being the Nine Ladies Stone Circle, with the accompanying King Stone. The stone circles placed high up on the moor had obvious connotations of worship and this continues today, when people gather to celebrate the winter and summer solstice on Stanton Moor. The similarly named Nine Stone Close on Harthill Moor is perhaps one of the best preserved of all the tall standing stone circles, even though it is missing some of the original standing stones and is set on private land.

Cairns are so numerous they dot the White Peak like snowflakes falling on the ground. All the ancient monuments increase in number as you move further south from the northern boundary, but even on Eyam Moor you can find a stone circle and cairn field.

Taddington church in a winter setting (Walk 13)

As the Iron Age dawned, settlements began to raise defences against both human and animal invasion. Fin Cop has a violent history that has only recently come to light, following excavation of the site.

As the Iron Age drew to a close, the Romans arrived and developed the communication and access around the area. Roman roads were famously straight, and a fine example is today's A515 which follows the route of the original Roman road between Buxton and Ashbourne. Another road, now lost, was called The Street and it ran from Buxton to the settlement of Derventio, near Derby. Navio, the Roman fort at Hope, connected with Melandra, near Glossop. In 2017 the remains of a small Roman settlement, including a Roman villa, was uncovered at Carsington, a truly exciting find.

Following the retreat of the Roman Empire, the area played host to a succession of rulers and tribes. The Pecsaete people, from whom the Peak area possibly takes its name, were absorbed into the Kingdom of Mercia that stretched from the mouth of the Humber to the southern coast of England. For administrative purposes land was divided into 'wapentakes', each one ensuring that laws were adhered to and taxes collected. Today the wapentake can be seen in action at the Barmote Court in Wirksworth that still sits to discuss mining claims. As prosperity grew, settlements were becoming established either around a nucleus or along linear lines that followed the characteristics of the land. These two types can still be seen in the villages of the White Peak; Sheldon is a fine example of a linear village, while Bakewell, now a bustling market town, is a good example of a settlement growing around a nucleus (the river crossing).

At the start of the second millennium, the arrival of the Norman's brought about a huge shift in Britain. The limestone plateau was originally common land with turbary rights for peat cutting. Small farmsteads were situated on the plateau and these can still be seen today. Many settlements date back well before the Norman period and some are mentioned in the Doomsday Book as well-established communities. Most villages are built of local limestone, with many of the buildings constructed from the 17th century onwards. However, the focal point of a village is a church, often with Norman origins particularly in the tower and around the doorway.

By studying the church it is often possible to decipher the development of the settlement. Many churches have features dating from periods subsequent to their original Norman construction. Doorways and windows are often useful for dating successive changes. The Victorian craze for improvement is much in evidence in church interiors and many fine features were lost, to the detriment of the building. Nevertheless, a great deal of local history can still be elicited from time spent in a church, as well as the appreciation of some fine workmanship. Perhaps the best example is the church at Tideswell, so magnificent that it is known as the Cathedral of the Peak.

With the coming of Enclosure in the Middle Ages and the arrival of the monasteries as landowners, the farm granges were developed. These were large farm operations, often remote from the local community and frequently managed by lay farmers. The farms were used to rear livestock, predominantly sheep, whose wool was prized around the world.

Lanes that once gave access to common land were now used to connect farmsteads and villages. Eventually, under Enclosure, the lanes acquired stone walls and became a defined right of way. A good example is the lane that runs across the wonderfully named Silly Dale, en route between the villages of Foolow and Wardlow Mires.

The wealth that wool and then lead mining brought into the area expanded the communities. For some it was a short-lived experience: the market town of Winster at the height of the lead-mining boom had approximately 2000 inhabitants; today they number around 580. But during the heyday, many settlements built fine churches and municipal buildings. Ashbourne is good example of excellent Georgian development of housing and commercial buildings.

The late 18th century and early 19th century brought the Industrial Revolution and all the changes that generated for society. Centred initially around Cromford and the mills of Sir Richard Arkwright, the Industrial Revolution changed the face of Britain. Millions of workers migrated from the fields and into the factories, and the social shape of the country had to change to accommodate all this new activity. This was a far cry from the quiet, secluded location of Cromford, chosen by the engineer as the place to establish his new system of working. Arkwright decided on Cromford firstly because of the available power supply: water could be harnessed to drive the mills. Secondly, the remote location enabled him to set up his factory in secret, so protecting his investment from destruction by weavers working in their own cottage workshops. The location also kept his plans secret from any competitors who might want to disrupt his business. Thirdly, he had a skilled workforce at hand and a reservoir of cheap labour from the fields to increase his production. The

The Headstone Viaduct crossing Monsal Dale (Walk 15)

enterprise was a success and soon he built further mills along the Derwent Valley. As the industry grew, other parties erected mills and soon the dales of the White Peak were ringing to the sound of cotton spinning day and night.

But a secluded location and access to water did not necessarily mean excellent communication links with the outside world. The area was still dominated by old routes and Roman roads to transport goods in and out. A new way had to be found and it came in three waves. First, the turnpike roads improved transport in and out of the factory locations. Their remnant can be seen today with tollhouses situated at strategic points, such as the one at Alport. But the quantity of goods transported was limited to the capacity of a horse and cart. The next wave saw the construction of several canals to bring in goods, such as coal. and transport the finished cotton to the weaving centres of the north. Finally, the railways arrived, speeding up transport and increasing trade; the railways also helped the growth of the major commercial and residential areas of the White Peak: Bakewell, Matlock and Ashbourne.

Many people did not welcome the arrival of the railways, perhaps the most famous being John Ruskin. Writing about the Bakewell to Buxton line that crosses the idyllic Monsal Dale via the beautiful Headstone Viaduct, Ruskin proclaimed:

There was a rocky valley between Buxton and Bakewell, once upon a time, divine as the Vale of Tempe... You Enterprised a Railroad through the valley – you blasted its rocks away, heaped thousands of tons of shale into its lovely stream. The valley is gone, and the Gods with it; and now, every fool in Buxton can be in Bakewell in half an hour, and every fool in Bakewell at Buxton; which you think a lucrative process of exchange – you Fools everywhere.

Often the railways were seen as destroyers of natural beauty, and it must have been quite a shock to witness this new technology careering through the countryside. But now the passenger railways are gone and perhaps we are the worse for it, for they would have provided excellent access for walking. But all is not lost; the rail track beds live on as wonderful, safe trails for enjoying the countryside on foot, hoof and bike.

LOCAL COMMUNITIES

Farming, still a major industry in the area, employs many people in the rearing of livestock and growing of crops. The technology may have changed and so has the number of people employed, but the landscape remains the same as it did after the Middle Ages and the end of ridge and furrow agriculture.

Quarrying is perhaps the largest industrial activity these days, the need

Ridge and furrow field system (Walk 32)

for limestone seemingly knowing no end. As you follow the walks in this book you will come across some of the quarries and, if you keep your ears open, you'll hear the warning siren followed by the muffled 'whump' of blasting. Quarries are dangerous places of work so never ever enter one.

The other major industry in the White Peak is tourism. The great estates such as Chatsworth draw millions of visitors a year, while the traditional 'well dressing' ceremonies that many of the villages still honour draw thousands more. Market day in Bakewell is still a significant event, as is the Shrovetide Tuesday football match through the streets of Ashbourne. And, of course, there is the landscape and scenery and all those walks to enjoy.

The creation of Britain's first national park in the Peak created a safe haven for the protection of the natural beauty and wildlife of the area. It also made it a magnet for visitors, many of whom need accommodation. While this brings welcome revenue into the local community, it has also created something of a problem that is not unique to this part of the country. The need for a holiday cottage, or worse, a second home, combined with the strict planning laws of a national park has removed a vast number of residential properties from local communities. Alongside this has been an increase in property prices, which are well beyond the resources of local people. The net effect of this dual pincer movement has meant the life has been driven out of small local villages and hamlets. The village store has gone, as have many of the pubs, and the vicar is now shared across many villages. This makes for a strange experience when walking through these places during the week. The quiet you sense as you move along the only street can be eerie. However, there are still pockets within the White Peak that retain much of their original community. Tissington is an excellent example, with its central street and shops dotted around the village, including a butcher and candlestick maker. Tissington is still populated by local inhabitants and draws tens of thousands of people to its well dressing ceremony every year. This state of affairs probably has much to do with the Fitzherbert family who have owned the village for over 500 years and still manage to keep it moving forward while retaining its original charm.

CUSTOMS

Local customs abound in the White Peak. Market day in Bakewell is a major event. Always on a Monday, the town bursts with activity from the cattle market, street stalls, pubs and cafés. Shrovetide Tuesday football in Ashbourne, when the 'Up'Ards' take on the 'Down'Ards', lasts all day or more. The term 'football' is used loosely to describe what is essentially a giant scrum from one end of town to the other. As it is played in Derbyshire, it is often cited as the origins of the term 'local derby'.

The greatest of all the local customs is the 'well dressing' that takes place in many of the villages each year. Local groups gather to make a tapestry out of flower petals pressed into clay and displayed by the village well for all to see.

Well dressing 2019, with Jimi Hendrix celebrating 50 years since Woodstock

In many of the older well dressings there is a significant pagan heritage. Wells were the only source of water for the community and the well dressing was a thank you to the gods for another year's supply. The biggest and most prominent display is in Tissington, where the ceremony takes place each year on the eve of Ascension Day. Tapestry themes vary enormously. Many are based on biblical themes, some offer commentary on national or world events, others commemorate great achievements both on the world stage and in the local community. Money collected from visitors throwing coins into the wells goes to help charities.

There are also some newer local customs; the more bizarre seem to be the most successful. The Bonsall Hen Race is held each year to growing acclaim and crowds. Betting on the races adds a sense of inclusion for many onlookers. The 'pecking' order of the hens is a closely guarded secret and 'fowl' play is carefully watched for to prevent any nobbling of the favourite bird.

At Fenny Bentley you can attend the World Toe Wrestling Championship, where opponents lock toes and try to pin the other's foot down. The winner receives his prize on the 'todium'. The defeated competitors can only stare at their inadequacy in shame.

The Sycamore Inn and village shop in Parwich (Walk 31)

PEAK DISTRICT NATIONAL PARK

Today the national park is fighting against growing cuts in funding and the need to protect the environment against continued and expanding commercial exploitation. Its ability to act as protector of this landscape is stretched to the limit and we all should do what we can to show our support. Perhaps the biggest challenge will be its response to climate change, the effects of which can be seen in the rivers of the White Peak, where the stepping stones across many are often totally submerged or have had to be raised more than once to keep people's feet dry. Maybe this is a simplification, but perhaps it is one of many signs we should take note of. The landscape will always be there, changing over time, yes, but that time stretches over millions of years and not just the few thousand that we have been around.

In an effort to raise much-needed money, the national park has had to become more commercial. Its focus on outreach and education is now more at the forefront. Its visitor centre in the town of Bakewell has a wealth of information about the area and the activities of the rangers and staff.

LOCAL SERVICES AND TRANSPORT

The two main centres of commerce in the White Peak, Bakewell and Matlock, are both useful as bases from which to explore the area. Wirksworth is another good option. Public transport relies mainly on local bus services; the railways are now leisure trails, although trains still run to Matlock station from Derby. Bus transport is available from the surrounding major cities of Manchester, Sheffield, Derby and Nottingham. Details of transport can be found at www.peakdistrict.gov.uk/visiting/publictransport.

Accommodation is part of most people's holiday break and numerous options are available in the White Peak, including camping, hostels, B&Bs and hotels. There is no wild camping allowed within the area. Details of accommodation can be found at www.visitpeakdistrict.com/accommodation.

THE WALKS

The walks in this book are covered by the eastern sheet of the Ordnance Survey White Peak map OL24, with a little added to cover Ashbourne in the south as this is a major gateway to the area, and the Hope Valley in the north to give walkers a taste of the Dark Peak. Choosing to keep the vast majority of walks within the eastern sheet will, I hope, make life a little easier for map readers; no more folding and unfolding as you try to find out which side Tideswell is on, or indeed where it is. Walks on the western sheet of the Ordnance Survey White Peak map OL24 will be covered in *Walking in the Peak District – White Peak West*.

One of the difficulties in designing these walks is the small area of open access, meaning walkers are restricted to public rights of way. I have endeavoured to keep away from roads, but this has not always been possible.

RESPONSIBLE WALKING

Always follow the countryside code. Close gates behind you. Do not climb over the drystone walls. Do not light fires. These are the basic instruction we all follow, I am sure. If a walk takes you across open access land it would be well worth checking before setting off that access is available. You can do this at www.openaccess.naturalengland.org.uk.

It is useful to leave a route of where you are going and what time you will return with a responsible person. If you do need help due to injury, dial 999 and ask for police/mountain rescue and have details of your location at the ready.

Dovedale from the summit of Thorpe Cloud (Walk 34)

Parking can be a problem on busy days. Try at all times to park in designated car parks and do not block field access or the minor roads in the area.

Although many of the walks pass through places where food and drink can be purchased – after all what better way to complete a walk than with lunch at a country pub – it is always advisable to carry food and drink with you.

Let me issue one word of caution: although the walking is generally gentle with the odd steep ascent or descent, limestone can be treacherous when wet, so take time and care.

MAPS AND NAVIGATION

The best map for the area is the Ordnance Survey White Peak OL24 1:25000. OL1 Dark Peak and OS Explorer 259 would also be useful. The Harvey/BMC White Peak 1:40000 has a wealth of information and covers the area well. Smartphone apps are now becoming more prevalent in their use. The GPX files of the walks are available for download from the Cicerone website.

While signposts and fingerposts are useful, a compass can always ensure you are walking in the right direction.

USING THIS GUIDE

I have split the guide into northern and southern sections, placing the dividing line between north and south near the village of Rowsley, the fold in the OS24 map. This seemed sensible and again stops the map from flying out of your hand while on the top of Thorpe Cloud. Walk 1 takes you along the boundary of the White and Dark Peak areas, giving you a glimpse of the northern wilderness available for future exploration using *Dark Peak Walks*. Walk 41 ends at Ashbourne, the southern gateway to the area, and offers you sight of what is to come in *Walking in the Peak District – White Peak West*.

The walks cover a variety of distances. Some are suitable for a morning stroll; many are for a full day of enjoyment. Where possible I have gathered walks around a central place to give holiday walkers a choice and also to allow them to become familiar with a location and therefore be able to appreciate it better. Many of the walks can be doubled up to make a longer day, and the four long walks can make up a wonderful weekend of exploration.

The walking times are based on traditional methods of calculation. However, when walking in large groups timings can quickly fall to the wayside. This is mainly due to stiles. The White Peak has thousands of them: one walk has a section with 31 stiles in a row. Getting a group through can take time, especially when a spring-loaded gate accompanies a squeeze stile. Allow for extra time on the walks if your walking party is large.

Having a dog on a lead is important in the White Peak but it can make squeeze stiles a challenge (Walk 31)

Because of the large number of stiles, the walk directions in places are simplified for clarity. For example, you might see an instruction to follow the path across fields SW for 1 mile (1.6km). Expect to find stiles, lots of them. Sometimes I give a little more detail by telling you how many stiles to go through. But telling you to go through 31 individual stiles does not make for brevity or interesting reading.

Similarly, for the 7 long walks and trails economy has been used in the route description to avoid an unduly lengthy section of the book. These routes are well signposted and clearly visible on OS 1:25000 maps. The GPX file is also available via the publishers website for download to a suitable device.

This guide includes an overview map and route summary table; use these along with the walk summary to select a suitable area for the day. Ordnance Survey 1:50000 maps accompany each of the day walks, while the longer walks and trails are covered by 1:100000 scale mapping in order to show the whole route. The place names and features marked in bold within the walk descriptions are marked on the map and should be used as an aid to navigation.

GPX tracks

GPX tracks for the routes in this guidebook are available to download free at www.cicerone.co.uk/976/GPX. A GPS device is an excellent aid to navigation, but you should also carry a map and compass and know how to use them. GPX files are provided in good faith, but neither the author nor the publisher accepts responsibility for their accuracy.

NORTHERN SECTION

The ancient Lady's Cross on White Edge Moor (Walk 4)

INTRODUCTION

The walks covering the northern section of this guide place you at the boundary of two very different landscapes. The walks straddle the edge of both the Dark Peak gritstone landscape of the high moorlands of the north and the pastoral farming landscape of the limestone White Peak. The communities that developed in the gritstone of the northern area are large and more concentrated in the valleys. These were formed 300 million years ago as the land mass was travelling north and the great river that we now know as the Rhine spilled out its sandy sediment into the delta that was to become the Derwent Valley.

Walking along the moorland paths above Eyam will give you a sense of what it is like to walk in the high moorlands of the Dark Peak that you can see wrapping around you to the north and east. There are some beautiful ancient woodlands to walk through, welcome on a hot day in late spring or early summer when the air is thick with the aroma of wild garlic and woodland bluebell. The walks around Grindleford and Longshaw are particularly good for this.

To the west you get your first taste of the deep limestone dales that thread through the White Peak. Towering limestone cliffs march along almost vertical slopes to give a feeling of enclosure and seclusion as you walk beside a crystal-clear stream. The dales are full of wildflowers in spring, rafts of colour heralding the rebirth of nature.

Evidence of ancient history seems to increase as you progress south through the area. Stanton Moor has a wonderful stone circle and so many other ancient sites that it attracts a large gathering during the summer and winter solstice. Ancient artefacts abound in the area and make for an interesting focal point for a walk. The great estate of Chatsworth with its grand house and gardens set in Capability Brown parkland is a magnet for people interested in art and cultural history. The house contains many precious works of art while the gardens, planned by Joseph Paxton of Crystal Palace fame, are a pleasure to sit and relax in.

The largest town in the White Peak is Bakewell, a must visit on a Monday when the traditional market is in full swing. This is a farming community so, along with the stalls selling everything from original Bakewell pudding to wooden clothes pegs, you will find prize sheep and cattle being auctioned.

WALK 1
Bradwell to Offerton

Start/Finish	St Barnabas Church, Bradwell SK 174 810
Distance	12 miles (19km)
Ascent/Descent	755m
Time	6hr
Terrain	Minor roads, open fields, footpath, trails and moorland
Map	OS 1:25000 Explorer OL24 White Peak, OS Explorer OL1 Dark Peak
Refreshments	Bradwell
Parking	Bradwell, on-street parking

Bradwell sits astride the Dark and White Peak. Geologically this is gritstone and limestone country. The walk from this typical Peak District village with its narrow lanes and huddled houses requires a little stamina at the beginning, but the reward is magnificent. If you have never walked across a moor before, then Offerton Moor will be a new experience that will entice you to venture further into the Dark Peak at a later date.

Starting from St Barnabas Church, walk SE along the **B6049**, and take the next road left, opposite the Shoulder of Mutton pub. Continue along the narrow road to The Green. Bear left down Bessie Lane to Edge Lane then ascend to a public bridleway. Follow the bridleway signpost through a gate and, after passing a stone gatepost on your right, leave the bridleway and take the footpath right to a squeeze stile at the junction of two walls. Follow the line of the wall right, through a metal gate onto **Bradwell Edge**. Cross a field to go through a second squeeze stile at a wall junction then follow the footpath past a dewpond on your left and the remains of **Robin Hood's Cross** by the wall on the right. At the end, go through a metal gate and over a stone stile into Brough Lane.

Once onto the moor there are fine **views of the northern Dark Peak**. To the northwest, the mass of Kinder Scout sits beyond the Great Ridge; in the north are the waters and gritstone edges of the Upper Derwent Valley; and to the east, the line of Stanage Edge fringes the skyline.

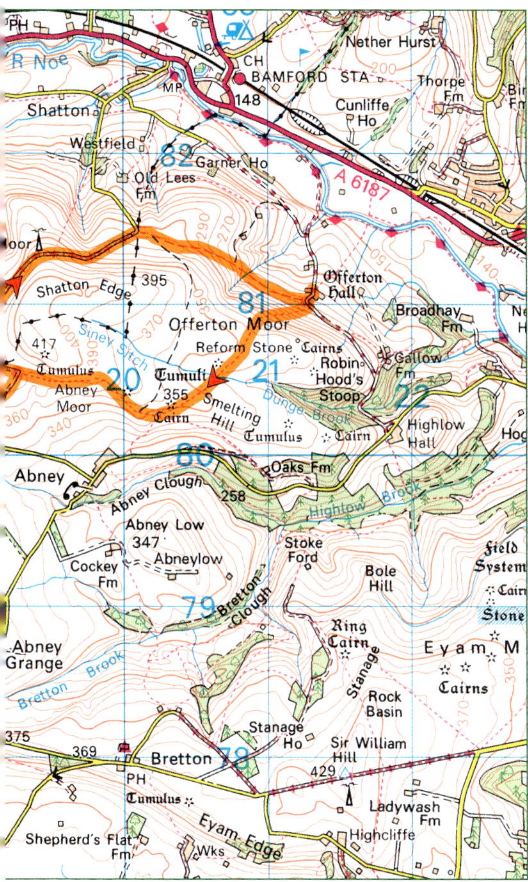

Turn right to go through a metal gate and proceed along Brough Lane, ignoring all side footpaths. Cross the wooden stile just after the lane to Abney and continue along the track through a farm gate. As it sweeps left then descends to the right it brings you to a metal farm gate. Go through and follow the track through another gate then pass the communication mast on **Shatton Moor**.

The view from Bradwell Moor to Kinder Scout

Further on, where the track becomes a road on a sharp left bend, follow the bridleway right, through the wooden farm gate and across fields. Keeping the wall on your left, walk along the bridleway until you reach the farm gate leading onto the road at **Offerton Hall**.

Go through the gate onto the road and take the stile immediately right to follow the footpath uphill onto **Offerton Moor**. Follow the moorland path SW across Offerton Moor, crossing a wooden footbridge over **Siney Sitch** and through a gate in a stone wall to a footpath sign, number 456, placed there, on **Smelting Hill**, by the Peak and Northern Footpath Society (PNFS).

These **Peak and Northern Footpath Society** signs can be found all over the Peak District. Beautifully made they are often a welcome confirmation that you are in fact on the right path. For over 100 years the society has kept a watchful eye on all the footpaths and, where attention is required, it liaises with the appropriate authority.

Take the footpath to Bradwell crossing two stiles to return to Brough Lane. Turn left and retrace your steps from earlier in the day. Crossing over the stile, passing the lane to Abney and then, where the track sweeps right, take the footpath left over the wall onto **Abney Moor**. Follow the undulating footpath across the moor to the road above **Abney Grange**. ▶

Go over a stile and turn right along the road. Where the tarmac track to Abney Grange meets the road take the footpath through the gate on your left. Cross the field opposite **Camphill** diagonally to the top left-hand corner, go through a second gate to follow a wall line down to a small stream. Go over the stream and follow the fence line SW past an abandoned house. Cross a second stream keeping SW uphill to a gate by a small underground reservoir then exit onto a road. Go left down the road to where the woodland starts and take the footpath right, down to the local school, then follow the lane into **Great Hucklow**.

Turn right through the centre of the village, pass the Queen Anne pub and take the lane on your right. Where the lane splits take the right-hand fork through the gate. Follow the farm track through a second gate to a signpost where the track turns uphill to the right. Follow the signpost going over the stile on the right at the junction of two walls, then cross fields, keeping the fence line on your right, to a second stone stile in the corner. Cross the stile then walk diagonally NW to pass through a gate and follow the fence line down to another gate. Go through the gate and down the field to the left-hand corner of a large industrial building and a PNFS sign. Follow the footpath along the side of a building through two metal gates to a

At this stage of the walk you may encounter a strange whirring noise. This is the gear winching a glider into the sky.

The Peak and Northern Footpath Society signs are a helpful and often welcome indicator of direction across the moors

tarmac lane leading to **Quarters Farm**. Turn left down the lane to the B6049.

Turn right, along the **B6049** and at the entrance to **Hazelbadge Hall Farm** cross the road and ascend Green Dale to a tarmac lane. Turn right then, when the lane sweeps sharp right, go left up Jennings Dale. Go through the gate at the top and turn right along **Earl Rake** then immediately left and ascend through woodland to a wooden stile to enter a field. Walk up through the field and where the path enters open ground follow its course to cross a stone stile. Go left along the wall line to a road. Turn right along the road the right again down the lane to **Hartlemoor Farm**. Halfway along the lane, take the stile on your left over a wall and across a field to a second stile, then turn right and follow the fenced footpath around the limestone quarry to a road. Turn right down the road and then take the footpath next left down to a wooden power pylon. Turn right here and follow the path down to a tarmac road. Turn right then immediately left through a squeeze stile and follow the footpath to return to **Bradwell**.

Bradwell Cottages

WALK 2
Hope to Shatton

Start/Finish	St Peter's Church, Hope SK 172 835
Distance	5.5 miles (9km)
Ascent/Descent	200m
Time	3hr
Terrain	Minor country roads, open fields, footpath
Map	OS 1:25000 Explorer OL1 Dark Peak
Refreshments	Hope
Parking	Hope SK 171 834

This short walk passes through some of the ancient villages that sit either side of the gritstone/limestone divide as well as visiting the remains of the Roman fort of Navio. The gentle stroll across the valley pastures is perfect for an afternoon foray or pre Sunday lunch outing. There are fine views along the valley and the gritstone edges of Kinder Scout, Bamford and Stanage.

From St Peter's Church in **Hope**, walk N down Edale Road passing on your right the only remaining dwelling from Birchinlee (Tin Town). ▶ Where the road forks, bear right to continue past a barn on your left to a track leading to a fenced lane. Walk down the lane to the house, go diagonally left across the yard and ascend steps into a field. Follow the footpath through the gate along the side of the hedge, over a stile and, after the second gate, turn left up the field to go beneath the rail bridge via a white gate. Turn right through two gates into a field. Walk diagonally right across the field and exit via a gate onto the lane directly below Farfield Farm. Turn right past the farm to a minor road junction, then go left towards **Aston**.

Before entering Aston, where the road crosses a stream, go right through a farm gate marked Kiln Croft and walk through another gate along the front of the houses following the left-hand fence. After the houses

Tin Town was built to house the workers who constructed the Derwent Valley dams.

pass through three gates and finally a squeeze stile to reach a road. Turn right passing Aston Hall on your left then after 600 metres to take the footpath left over a stone stile into fields. Follow the field boundary on your right passing through six gates or stiles to arrive at a farm gate leading onto a driveway. Go across the drive and through the farm gate opposite, then across fields, generally E, going through a squeeze stile and a gate to exit via a final gate in front of cottages onto a minor road. Turn left and then take the first footpath right by the corner of a house leading into woodland. Proceed over a stile down the wooded hillside to arrive at a road with a house on your left.

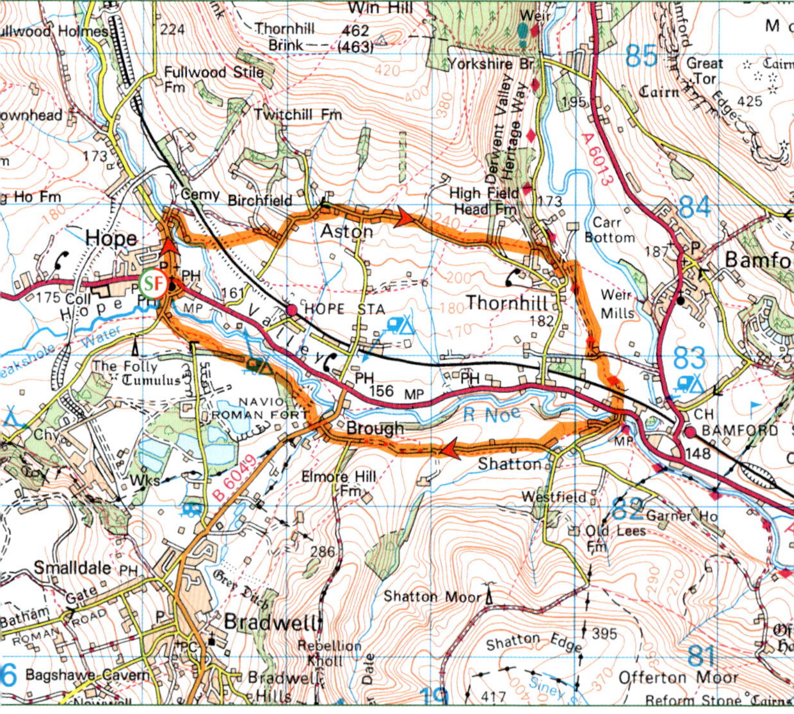

Old trees often mark ancient routes across the landscape

Go through the gate and cross the road to a gate opposite to walk down a field and through a gate onto the **Thornhill Trail**. ▶

Go right along the trail passing through a wide gate until the trail meets a road. Go left and, opposite the Quaker Community house, go right over the stile into a field.

Have a good look at the **Quaker Community house**. Above the door you will see the initials DVWB. This used to be the head office of the Derwent Valley Water Board, the body responsible for the construction of the Upper Derwent reservoirs. It was this body that built Tin Town in the Upper Derwent Valley to house workers constructing the Derwent and Howden dams.

Follow the footpath to a second gate and exit the field onto a lane. Turn right under a railway bridge then continue straight ahead to the **A6187**. Cross the road and

The Thornhill Trail is the bed of the railway line that brought stone from the Grindleford quarries up to the Upper Derwent Valley to construct the Howden and Derwent dams.

go over the stone bridge leading to **Shatton**, then take the first road right, marked as a private road. At the top of this road go over the stile into a field and follow the footpath W across two stiles and down stone steps onto Townfield Lane. Ascend the stone steps opposite and turn right through the gate to follow the footpath through a gate right of a barn onto a road. Where the road meets a cattle grid go right through the farm gate and follow the track uphill carrying straight on, ignoring the turn-off to Upper Shatton. Go through two gates and down the lane to emerge onto a road leading into **Brough**. Walk down the road to the junction with the **B6049** and the Roman Batham Gate.

> **Navio Fort** was a Roman policing outstation that sat at the centre of a network of major communication routes. Batham Gate ran from the fort at Templeborough in Yorkshire to Navio then onto the spa baths at Buxton. A second route ran from Navio over the moors via Doctor's Gate to Ardotalia (Melandra), the fort at Glossop. Navio was constructed around 80BC and was in use until around AD2. Originally built to protect the lead mining interests and the access up the Hope Valley, it was also near springs that may have proved to be of medicinal value. Little is left of the fort now except the outline of the base that can clearly be seen.

Turn left and cross the wooden footbridge then right through the gate to take the public footpath to Hope. After crossing the **Roman Fort of Navio** descend to cross the wooden footbridge then turn left over the stile and follow the tree boundary downhill across fields. As it becomes a sunken lane you go through a squeeze stile and pass the remains of an ancient cross. Continue until you reach a stile leading onto a road. Go right down the road to a junction, then right again over a footbridge near the village pinfold. Take the next right and return to the church at **Hope**.

WALK 3

Longshaw to Curbar Gap

Start/Finish	Longshaw Estate SK 264 799
Distance	10 miles (16km)
Ascent/Descent	520m
Time	5hr
Terrain	Minor country roads, footpath and trail
Map	OS 1:25000 Explorer OL24
Refreshments	National Trust visitor centre, Longshaw Estate
Parking	Longshaw Estate SK 266 800

Longshaw, the former hunting estate of the Duke of Rutland is now in the hands of the National Trust. The walk through the estate is a pleasant ramble with excellent views to Kinder Scout and beyond as you progress onto Froggatt and Curbar edges. These lines of gritstone are famed for their rock climbs and wonderful views. The edges also have a wealth of industrial heritage with the millstone quarries that lined the face still showing evidence of their former activity.

Setting off from the front of **Longshaw Lodge**, walk SW along a sunken path, called a ha-ha.

> The **ha-ha** was constructed to provide a continual view of parkland from the shooting lodge while at the same time creating a barrier to livestock. The pasture beyond the ha-ha is where the Longshaw Sheepdog Trials take place every year in September, attracting large crowds of spectators. Having been staged there since 1898, the organisers claim they are the oldest trials in the country.

Go through the gate and then a second gate immediately after to join a well-made wide track heading through another gate SW towards the Grouse Inn. After

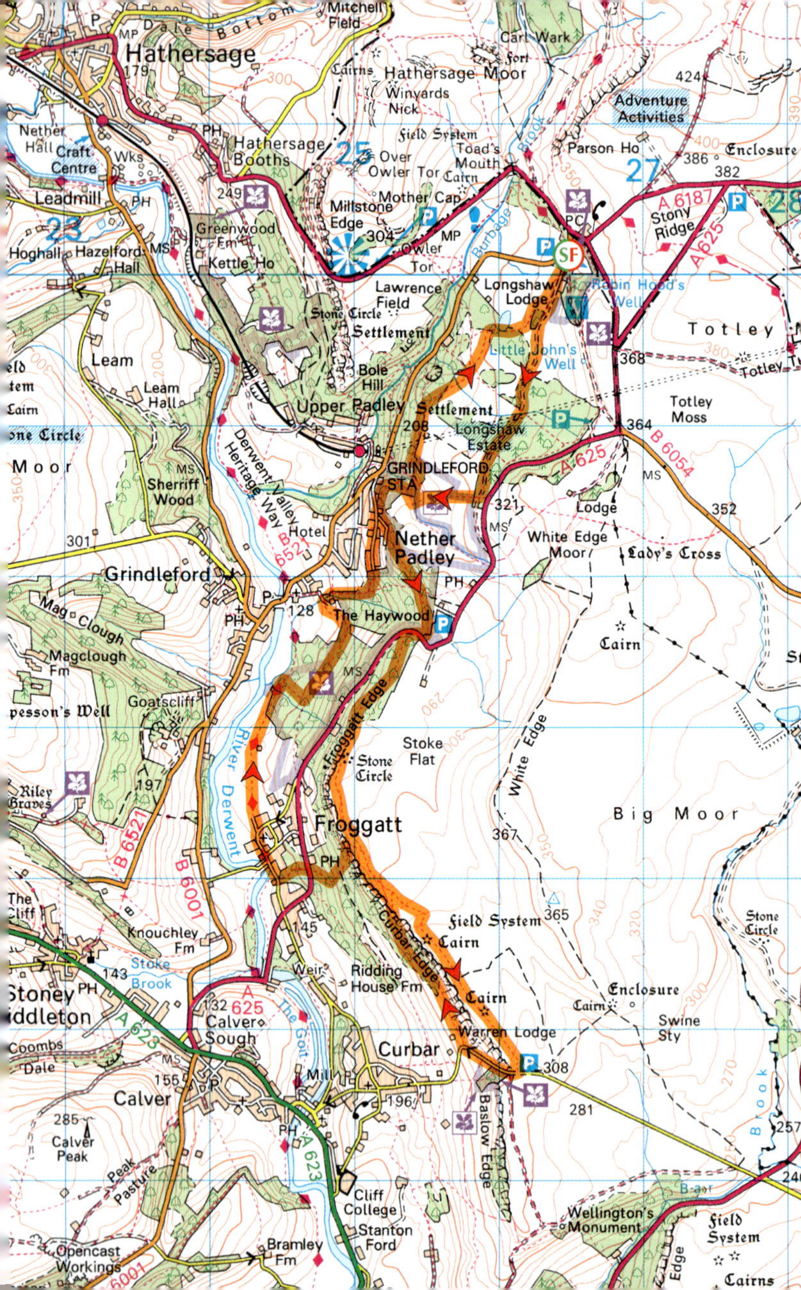

Hathersage
Mitchell Field
Carl Wark
fort
Hathersage Moor
Winyards Nick
Cairns
Adventure Activities
Parson Ho
Nether Hall Craft Centre
Wks
Hathersage Booths
Toad's Mouth
Over Owler Tor
Field System
PC
Stony Ridge
Enclosure
Leadmill
PH
Greenwood Fm
Mother Cap
Millstone Edge
Owler Tor
Hoghall
Hazelford Hall
MS
Kettle Ho
Longshaw Lodge
Robin Hood's Well
Totley
Lawrence Field
Leam
Stone Circle
Settlement
Little John's Well
Totley
Leam Hall
Bole Hill
Upper Padley
Settlement
Longshaw Estate
Totley Moss
MOOR
Sherriff Wood
Derwent Valley Heritage Way
GRINDLEFORD STA
Lodge
White Edge Moor
Lady's Cross
one Circle
Hotel
NETHER PADLEY
Grindleford
Mag Clough
The Haywood
PH
Magclough Fm
Goatscliff
MS
Froggatt Edge
Stoke Flat
White Edge
Big Moor
pesson's Well
River Derwent
Stone Circle
Riley Graves
Froggatt
PH
Cairn
Curbar Edge
Field System
The Cliff
Knouchley Fm
Stoke Brook
Cairn
Stone Circle
Stoney Middleton
Weir
Ridding House Fm
Cairn
Enclosure
Coombs Dale
Calver Sough
Warren Lodge
Swine Sty
Calver
Curbar
Mill
Baslow Edge
Calver Peak
Peak Pasture
Cliff College
Stanton Ford
Wellington's Monument
Field System
Opencast Workings
Bramley Fm
Cairns

1 mile (1.5km) take the footpath on the right across open moor until you reach a stream on the edge of woodland. Go left across the stepping-stones to the walled corner of woodland and follow the wall across a stream and up a steep bank to enter a walled lane. Go right through the gate in the wall and take the woodland path, which then becomes a lane behind houses after passing through a gate. Go through a gate at the bottom and, where the lane meets a road, go left then immediately left again and, after passing through a gate, follow the footpath up through **The Haywood**. At the top, bear right to cross a stream then exit onto the **A625** via a stone stile. Cross the road and go through the gate leading up onto **Froggatt Edge**. ▶

Walk along the edge path until it descends through a gate to the road at Curbar Gap car park. Turn right and walk down the road until you reach a sharp left-hand bend. Take the footpath on the right and follow this up through the boulder field to emerge on top of **Curbar Edge** then go NW until the edge path forks. Take the left-hand

Just as you reach Froggatt Edge there is a beautiful Bronze Age stone circle and field system to the left of the path.

The stone circle on Froggatt Edge

fork down and walk along the bottom of the crag, taking note of the dished millstones awaiting collection.

From the millstones take the footpath S down through trees and gate, emerging onto a road. Go straight across and continue downhill until you meet a minor road in the village of **Froggatt**. Go right, through the village to the junction with Spooner Lane. Walk along

FROGGATT EDGE MILLSTONES

Millstones at the quarry on Froggatt Edge

Below Froggatt Edge lay a quarry that produced millstones that were used for grinding grain for bread and feed. French millstones were favoured for the processing of flour for wheat, as British stones produced grey flour that was unfashionable to the palates of the higher classes. Southern England provided a large market for Peak District stones. The price for each stone at the beginning of the 14th century was 16s 1¼d (81p), a cost that remained stable until the arrival of the Black Death that decimated the population in the middle of the century. By the end of the century the cost of a Peak millstone had risen to 32s (160p), in large part due to the lack of available labour to both produce and use the millstones.

the walled lane then follow the footpath across fields to enter Froggatt Wood via a small squeeze stile. Keep on the stone-flagged path through the wood until you come to a small signpost shortly after crossing a stream. Go right, up through the trees to a 'T' junction with another path running NE. Go left crossing a stream along the way then through a gap in a wall and across a second stream. Follow the path left down along plastic duckboards and through a gate into an open field. Follow the diverted footpath signs left then right, around the house, exiting via a gate onto a driveway. Walk left a few metres then go right, through a gap in a wall, then through a gate and walk up a steep woodland slope with a wall on your left. At the wall corner go left, then exit through a gate onto a minor road.

Go straight ahead then right at the end of houses on your right and walk uphill, retracing your steps from earlier in the day. At the top, go through the gate and left along the walled lane then drop down the slope and go straight ahead across the two streams and up through trees to a five-bar gate leading into Longshaw. Do not go through the gate but go left along the path, through a small gate then turn right. Follow the path, that works its way high above Grindleford, bearing right at all times until you reach a gate leading into the **Longshaw Estate**. Go through and follow the trail to a junction then go left and follow this to a small plantation of Scots pine. Go right, following the path through the trees and via a gate emerge by the pond below **Longshaw Lodge**. Go right again and follow the path back to the visitor centre.

WALK 4

Grindleford to White Edge

Start/Finish	Grindleford Station car park SK 251 787
Distance	8.5 miles (14km)
Ascent/Descent	390m
Time	4.5hr
Terrain	Footpaths, tracks, some exposed edges
Map	OS 1:25000 Explorer OL24
Refreshments	Grindleford Station
Parking	Grindleford Station car park SK 251 787

This walk starts at the famous Grindleford Station Café, known for its breakfasts and signs telling the customer what they can and cannot do. The walk explores the National Trust Longshaw Estate and the Eastern Moors. Both areas are managed for wildlife and these moors are a magnet for people interested in natural history. The area is also steeped in archaeology, with ancient crosses, hut circles and guide stoops.

From **Grindleford Station Café** walk across the rail bridge and follow the rough road until you come to a junction leading to a steep hill with a sign pointing N to Longshaw Estate and Padley Gorge. Turn right here and walk up the hill and through the gate at the top to enter woodland.

Walk along the woodland path for 300 metres then take the right-hand path downhill, turning right at a stone seat as the path zigzags down to a wooden bridge across Burbage Brook. Cross the bridge, turn right and walk up steps and at the top bear left then up more steps through woodland. Where the path forks, keep right to emerge onto the **B6521** via a squeeze stile. Go diagonally left across the road and follow the signpost path S up through woodland. Where the path intersects a second path running E–W, turn left to enter the **Longshaw Estate** via a gate.

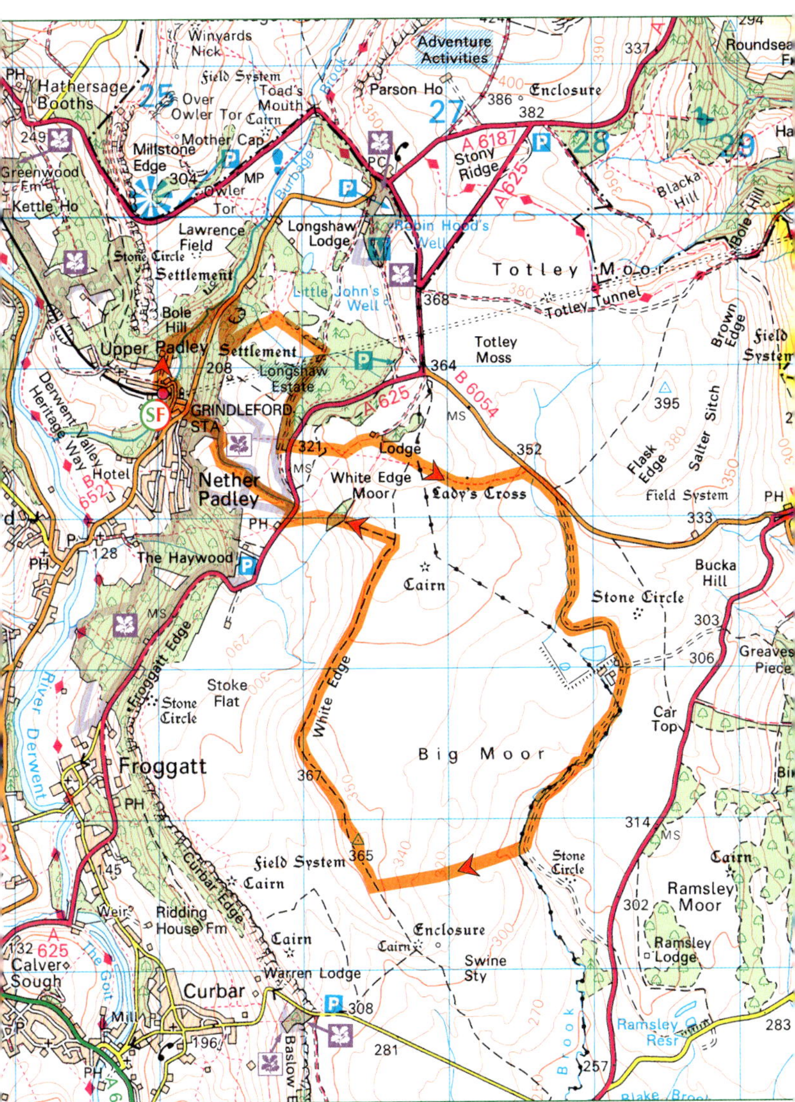

Winyards Nick
Adventure Activities
Roundsea
Hathersage Booths
Field System
Toad's Mouth
Parson Ho
Enclosure
Over Owler Tor
Cairn
Stony Ridge
Blacka Hill
Millstone Edge
Mother Cap
A 6187
Bole Hill
Greenwood Em
Owler Tor
Kettle Ho
Longshaw Lodge
Robin Hood's Well
Totley Moor
Lawrence Field
Settlement
Little John's Well
Totley Tunnel
Stone Circle
Brown Edge
Settlement
Bole Hill
Totley Moss
Field System
Upper Padley
Settlement
Longshaw Estate
Totley Moss
Salter Sitch
GRINDLEFORD STA
Flask Edge
Derwent Valley Heritage Way
Lodge
B 6054
A 625
Lady's Cross
White Edge Moor
Field System
Hotel
Nether Padley
Bucka Hill
The Haywood
Stone Circle
Cairn
Greaves Piece
Froggatt Edge
Stoke Flat
White Edge
Car Top
Stone Circle
Big Moor
Froggatt
Stone Circle
Field System
Cairn
Ramsley Moor
Ridding House Fm
Cairn
Enclosure
Ramsley Lodge
Calver Sough
Warren Lodge
Cairn
Swine Sty
Curbar
Baslow
Ramsley Resr
Mill
Curbar Edge
River Derwent
The Goit
Weir
Blake Brook

The **Longshaw Estate** was originally the hunting ground of the Duke of Rutland. The house began life as a small hunting lodge, growing in size and stature as the earnings from the grouse shoots increased. The whole estate is now in the hands of the National Trust. There are extensive walks, ranging from simple ambles along wide tracks to more adventurous explorations of the moors and woodlands.

Follow the grassy path NE until it meets a wide track. Turn right, walking SE up a gentle slope to a signpost for the Grouse Inn. Follow these directions through a gate until you reach open moorland on the right. Here, take the footpath on the left through a gate and squeeze stile to the **A625**. Go directly across the road then through a gate and walk straight ahead, rising gently up to a bridleway running to **White Edge Lodge**. At the lodge turn right and walk up to a gate on the horizon, keeping the woodland on your left. Go through the gate and slightly left, then take the footpath SE then E across **White Edge Moor**, passing the remains of an **ancient cross** on your right, until the track meets a farm gate leading onto **B6054**.

Like many of the crosses that stand upon the moors, **Lady's Cross** has both a religious and geographical purpose. The cross marks the boundary of the monastic lands of Beauchief Abbey in Sheffield. An important part of land management was a clear boundary definition. Over time the cross became a waymark for people travelling across the moor.

A keen eye will spot a wealth of wildlife here, including adder, water vole, great spotted woodpecker and curlew.

Turn right before the gate and walk across Bar Brook, keeping to the wall line until you meet a track running generally SE. Follow this track through a gate and around the perimeter of a dried-up reservoir bed, exiting the area via a farm gate. ◀

Keep walking straight ahead, crossing a tarmac drive and following the grass track at the other side through a farm gate. Pass a small pond on the right then shortly after, as the track sweeps left, leave it and go right to cross Bar Brook and walk up the narrow gully, passing an ancient marker post near to the top.

> There are two **stone circles** that can be visited on this walk. The largest and ironically hardest to detect sits just northeast, between the reservoir and a line of trees on the horizon. The second is sited just off the track southeast of the turning point to head for White Edge. This is more prominent and has excellent features. Both date from the late Neolithic/early Bronze Age period.

After reaching the marker post, aim for a short stone column in a SW direction across **Big Moor**. At the column carry on SW until you come to **White Edge**. Turn right and walk along the edge on the clear path, passing the **Ordnance Survey triangulation pillar** on your right, until you reach a wall.

THE COMPANION STONES

Around the walk you will come across recently carved stonework bearing words and poetry. These are the Companion Stones design by Jo Dacombe. They are modern-day companions to the ancient guideposts and ways that criss-cross this part of the Peak District. They do not point a way forward on land, but into the future. The poem carved around the stones on White Edge reads:

*for this ride / come out / ward hear / heath / er on air / step / on g /
rounded c / loud let / soul rotate / as hori / zon / walk sky / wards*

The Companion Stone on White Edge by Jo Dacombe with poetry by Mark Goodwin

Go through the gap in the wall and turn left, following the wall downhill to a fingerpost. Take the left-hand path down through a gate and across a small field and exit via a gate onto the **A625** by the Grouse Inn. Cross the road and turn right, walking up the road a short distance, then take the first footpath left through a gate onto the **Longshaw Estate**. Follow a track along the wall line until it sweeps left. Take the footpath on the right, down through rough pasture following the course of a stream until you reach a wall corner bounding woodland. Go right across the stream and up a short section of paved footpath. At the split in the grassy path take the left-hand fork leading through a gate downstream. Continue downhill along a rough path until, walking down stone steps, you emerge onto the **B6521**. Go diagonally left across the road to arrive back at **Grindleford Station**.

Woodland trails through Padley Gorge

WALK 5

Foolow to Wardlow

Start/Finish	Foolow SK 190 768
Distance	7 miles (11.5km)
Ascent/Descent	240m
Time	4hr
Terrain	Minor country roads, footpath, trail
Map	OS 1:25000 Explorer OL24
Refreshments	Foolow, Wardlow Mires
Parking	Foolow, on-street parking

Foolow is a pretty if quiet village providing good photo opportunities with its choice of duck pond, village green, ancient cross, manor house and country pub. As you enter Cressbrook Dale you pass through nature reserves and sites of special scientific interest (SSSIs), becoming aware of the limestone landscape that was carved out by the rivers millions of years ago. Geologically there is much to be seen in the towers of limestone and rock outcrops.

From the centre of **Foolow**, walk SW with the village pond on your right and take the walled footpath past the farmhouse and through the farm gate, then follow footpath directions aiming to the right of a large tree by a wall. Go through the gate and continue crossing eight walls by gate or stile until you enter a narrow lane with low walls. Cross the lane and two subsequent stiles until you reach the wonderfully named **Silly Dale**. ▶

The name Silly Dale is derived from the old word 'seely', meaning blessed or happy.

Go over the stone stile and enter the lane, turning right to Stanley House. Take the footpath to the right of the house entrance going over the stone stile and heading due S towards **Wardlow Mires**. Cross two stone stiles and enter the farm by three metal gates. Follow the route through the farmyard and emerge onto the **A623**. Go right, past the junction for Wardlow then cross the road to enter Cressbrook Dale.

Cressbrook Dale is a beautiful dale dominated by the massive bulk of Peter's Stone. Peter's Stone is often known as Gibbet Rock. Felons receiving the death sentence were hanged at Wardlow Mires and then displayed in chains on Gibbet Rock as a warning to passers-by. The dale floor can flood in wet weather, particularly around the northeastern end, so prepare to get wet boots. The dale is full of interesting plants and wildlife, including the early purple orchid that flowers between April and June.

Follow the footpath below **Peter's Stone** until you pass a small footbridge on your right leading to **Tansley Dale**. Keep SE on the public footpath to ascend the left-hand hillside to a stone stile at the top. Go over the stile and follow the wide, walled lane E, exiting via a squeeze

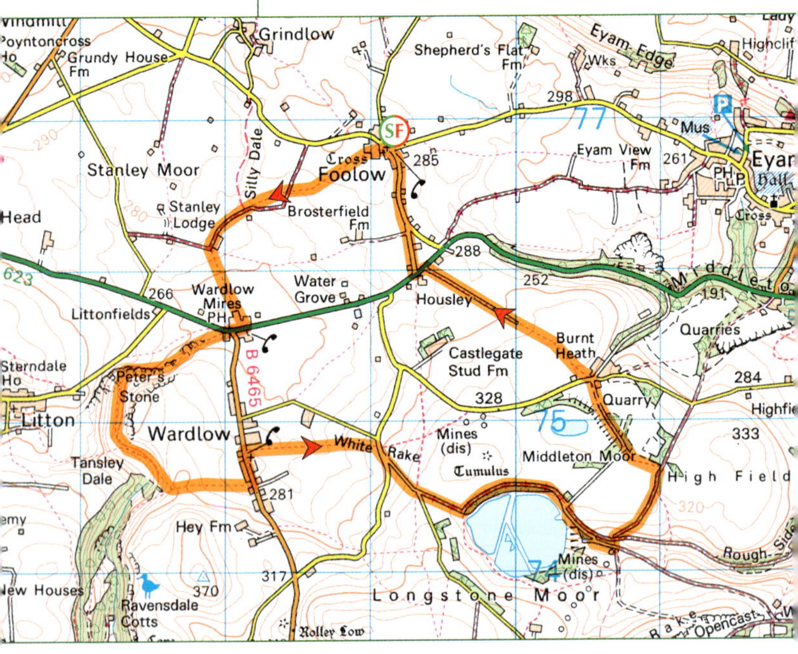

Storm clouds approaching Cressbrook Dale

stile onto the **B6465**. Cross the road and turn left into **Wardlow**. Just after the Church of the Good Shepherd take the footpath before the telephone box and head E across several fields, passing through five gates to the minor road by **White Rake**. Go right along the road and, where it forks, go left then left again at the second fork. Continue, as the surface becomes a rough track, skirting the northern edge of a **large pond** until you reach the crossing of two tracks E of the pond. Go N up the bridleway to your left until, reaching the top, you meet a footpath on the left by a high grassy bank. Go NW over the stile to follow the fingerpost along this path, then turn right on meeting a wide track and walk down the road to Glebe Mine's Cavendish Mill. ▶

The manufacture of products as diverse as asthma inhalers, mobile phones, toothpaste and unleaded petrol all rely on the fluorspar that comes out of Glebe Mine.

Go left at the junction and take the footpath on the right over the stone stile and then through three gates to cross **Burnt Heath** to a walled lane. Go NW along the lane to the road at **Housely**. Walk left, then cross the **A623** and take the next right. Walk along the minor road bearing left where it meets another and continue into **Foolow**.

WALK 6

Eyam to Abney

Start/Finish	Eyam car park SK 216 767
Distance	10 miles (16km)
Ascent/Descent	580m
Time	5hr
Terrain	Open fields, footpath, moorland
Map	OS 1:25000 Explorer OL24 White Peak
Refreshments	Eyam
Parking	Eyam SK 216 767

This route is full of ancient artefacts and significant historical places, starting with Eyam, the village famous for the plague that befell it in the 17th century. The views across the White Peak from Eyam Edge are unsurpassed in the Peak District. Bretton Clough is one of the national park's hidden delights and, close by, there's even a pub with incredible views.

From **Eyam** car park turn left down Hawkhill Road, past the museum then turn left at the junction and walk along Church Street. Where the road forks bear left into The Square. Go left at the next road junction and follow the road around a left-hand bend, then take Riley Back Lane on the left. Where the lane splits take the right-hand fork and follow the footpath up through woodlands.

At the next footpath junction, marked with a post, continue right, up through the woods to a squeeze stile leading onto Edge Road. Go right, passing the road to Bretton on the left, and walk a further 100 metres to arrive at **Mompesson's Well**.

Carry on along Edge Road until it turns sharp right and becomes Sir William Hill Road. Take the stone stile directly opposite the bend to reach the footpath marked Abney. Follow the wall line, keeping it on your right until you reach a stone squeeze stile. Go through and walk

MOMPESSON'S WELL

Mompesson's Well was named after William Mompesson who was vicar of Eyam during the outbreak of plague in the village. Several wells sited on the edge of the village were used to collect food from neighbouring villages. This protected the outside world from contagion. In his book, *My Heroes: Extraordinary Courage, Exceptional People*, Ranulph Fiennes lists the inhabitants of the plague-hit village as all being heroes for their sacrifice.

Mompesson's Well

across **Eyam Moor** to visit the cairn field and stone circle at Wet Withens. Retrace your steps to exit via the stile and continue right until the footpath swings left to the Peak and Northern Footpath Society signpost.

Turn right and follow the footpath, then go over a stone stile by a metal gate. Take the footpath along the wall line, going over another stone stile in the process. Eventually the path swings left and descends to **Stoke Ford**. Turn right to go across a footbridge spanning **Bretton Brook** and through the gate at the other side. Turn right, cross a second footbridge then follow the signpost left up through **Abney Clough** and four gates to emerge in **Abney village**. ◄

Turn left and walk through the village until you reach a footpath on the left signposted Nether Bretton. Follow this sign through a gate and down to a footbridge. Cross the brook then walk up a banking to go through a gate leading into a field. Follow the footpath left around the hillside. Go through a gate and walk up pasture to the top right corner. Go through another gate and over a stone stile and follow the footpath along a wall line to a farm track. Pass **Cockey Farm** on your right then veer right across a field. Go over a stone stile and a second one further on to gain a wooden stile opposite a small clump of trees with a bench seat. Follow the footpath down the hillside and across a wooden bridge then through a gate and across a second footbridge over **Bretton Brook**. Follow the footpath due S to an open area. Go W along the concession footpath through mounds that make it look like a lunar landscape.

It is well worth taking time to explore **Bretton Clough** for its geological features and the questions it raises. It is thought that a glacial process created the mounds and hummocks during the Devensian geological period. A combination of ground waters, ice and landslips produced what is now a complicated and fascinating geological puzzle of slide blocks and valleys.

Go through two gates along the path and, at the stone wall running N–S, go through another gate and follow the wall left up the hill. Cross the wall stile and the road to the signpost directly opposite. Descend the hillside S and, where the path intersects a second running E–W, go right. Pass Silence Mine on your left and emerge through a gate onto a road.

> **Silence Mine** is a good example of the layout of a deep lead mine. The shaft depth extended well beyond 150 metres and required pumping engines to extract the water. The mine did not produce great quantities of ore and, in 1886, the shaft collapsed, consuming as it did so many of the surface buildings. After that the mine was abandoned.

Go left down the road and after 350 metres take the footpath left across a wooden stile towards **Grindlow**. Cross over a wall and turn right to Rose Farm. At the farm go through the gate and bear left around the farm buildings to a low wall. Slip through the squeeze stile and walk diagonally across the small field to the stone stile by a signpost. Follow the driveway along the line of the wall on your left to the road. Go left and then immediately left again to walk down the footpath that starts between the stone barn and the wall. Follow the footpath SE across seven stiles or gates to reach the road, then head left to enter **Foolow**.

At the Bulls Head Inn go right, along the road to Housley. At the end of the houses on the left take the first footpath through a private yard to the stone stile, opposite. Go across the stile and follow the signpost across successive fields using a further 20 stiles or gates until you reach Tideswell Lane on the outskirts of Eyam. Go across the lane and through the gate opposite to follow the footpath across the field to a road. Cross the road slightly to the right to walk down a footpath leading out into a housing estate. Walk straight down through the estate to the junction of Church Street in the centre of **Eyam** and retrace your steps to the car park.

WALK 7

Eyam to Grindleford

Start/Finish	Eyam SK 216 767
Distance	11 miles (17.5km)
Ascent/Descent	600m
Time	5.5hr
Terrain	Footpath, moorland, woodland, open fields
Map	OS 1:25000 Explorer OL24 White Peak
Refreshments	Eyam
Parking	Eyam SK 216 767

This walk follows some of the places that have a connection with the plague that befell the village of Eyam, pronounced 'E'em', in the middle of the 1600s. Part of the walk through Froggatt Wood follows an old packhorse route along a paved causeway worn by millions of feet and hooves. The return journey from Grindleford over Eyam Moor gives wonderful views up into the Dark Peak area of the national park.

From **Eyam** car park, turn left down Hawkhill Road towards the centre of the village. Turn left at the junction and walk along Church Street. Where the road forks, bear left into The Square. Go left at the next road junction and follow the road around a left-hand bend then go right to Riley Lane. Where the lane forks take the left-hand route towards the **Riley Graves**.

> The **Riley Graves** are named after the location and not the name of a family. It is a sad story of pain and loss. During the plague that raged among the villagers in the 17th century, Elisabeth Hancock buried her husband and six children here in a period of just eight days.

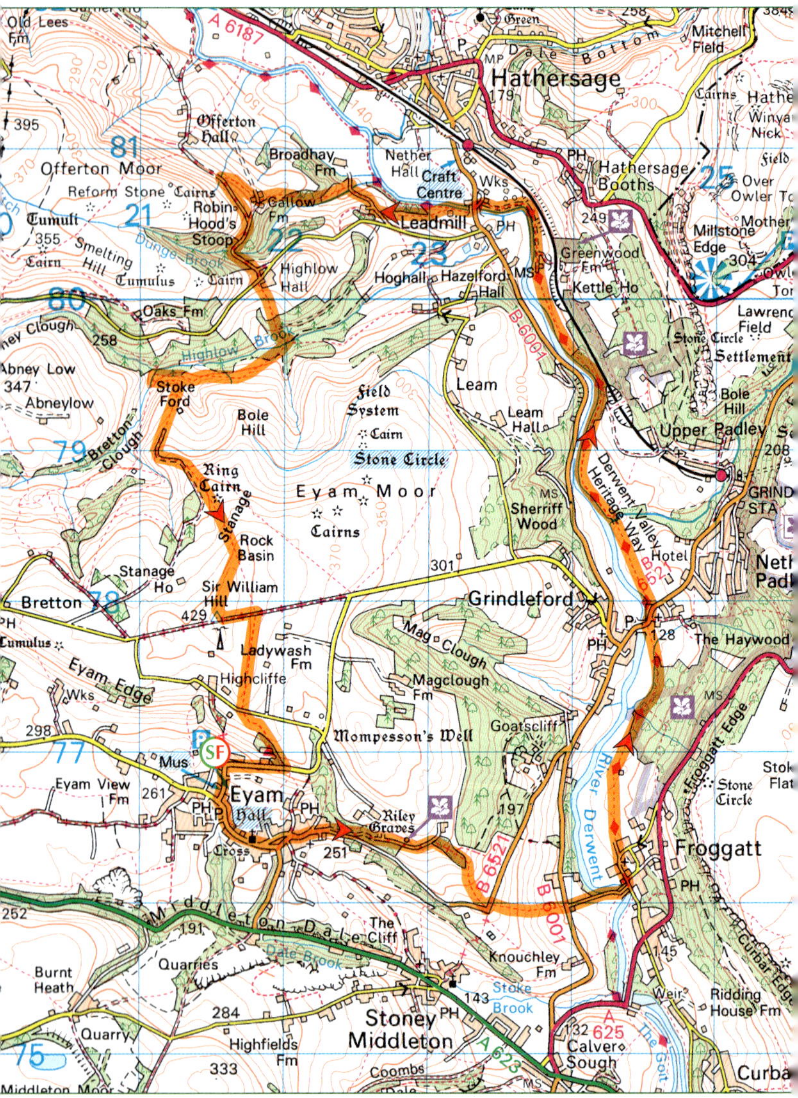

Old Lees Fm
Offerton Hall
Offerton Moor
Reform Stone
Robin Hood's Stoop
Gallow Fm
Broadhay Fm
Nether Hall
Craft Centre
Hathersage
Mitchell Field
Winyards Nick
Over Owler Tor
Millstone Edge
Mother
Hathersage Booths
Greenwood Fm
Kettle Ho
Leadmill
Highlow Hall
Hoghall
Hazelford Hall
Leam
Lawrence Field
Stone Circle
Settlement
Bole Hill
Upper Padley
Oaks Fm
Stoke Ford
Bole Hill
Field System
Cairn
Leam Hall
Bretton Clough
Stone Circle
Eyam Moor
Sherriff Wood
Derwent Valley Heritage Way
Hotel
Ring Cairn
Cairns
Rock Basin
Stanage
Sir William Hill
Stanage Ho
Bretton
Grindleford
Mag Clough
Magclough Fm
The Haywood
Ladywash Fm
Highcliffe
Eyam Edge
Goatscliff
Froggatt Edge
Stone Circle
Stoke Flat
Mompesson's Well
Eyam View Fm
Eyam
Eyam Hall
Riley Graves
Froggatt
River Derwent
Cross
Middleton Dale
The Cliff
Knouchley Fm
Curbar Edge
Burnt Heath
Quarries
Dale Brook
Stoke Brook
Ridding House Fm
Weir
Quarry
Highfields Fm
Stoney Middleton
Calver Sough
Coombs Dale
Curbar

At the fork in the lane take the right-hand lane down into woodland, keeping right at the next fork progressing down to a minor road. Go left then right through a gate at the bend in the road and descend fields, crossing two stiles to the **B6521**. Go straight across and follow the minor road across the packhorse bridge over the **River Derwent** into the village of **Froggatt**. Bear left through the village along Hollowgate until it sweeps right then join Spooner Lane, following the fingerpost for Grindleford Bridge. Keep on the lane, crossing fields and four stiles until you enter Froggatt Wood. Follow the packhorse route through the woodland into open pasture, cross a brook on the left and walk diagonally right until you reach the **Grindleford Bridge** on the **B6521**.

Go diagonally right across the road and enter open fields by the bridge. Follow the banks of the **River Derwent**, passing through Coppice Wood until you reach a gate leading onto a tarmac lane. Go left, passing through Harper Lees and a further gate eventually reaching **Leadmill** on the **B6001**. Go left, crossing Leadmill Bridge, then right through a gate into fields following the fingerpost for Shatton. Follow the footpath until you reach a derelict barn with a signpost close by. Go left following the signpost up through woodland via steps, over a stone stile and across the field, exiting via a gate to the lane leading to **Broadhay Farm**. Go right along the lane then immediately right again down a track. Just after passing over a stream, take the footpath left across a field to woodland. Enter the woods through a gate and exit via a gate crossing a field to **Callow Farm**. Go left along a farm track and, after leaving the farmyard, follow the signpost right, uphill to trees. Go into the woods through a gate; the path then crosses sloping fields to a stile onto a minor road. Go left, passing the **Robin Hood's Stoop** on your right until you reach a road junction. ▶

Turn right and follow the road, taking the right-hand fork up to reach **Highlow Hall**.

It is said that Robin Hood shot an arrow from this spot to land in the churchyard of Hathersage, marking the spot where his lieutenant Little John is buried.

Highlow Hall

Highlow Hall was the home of Robert Eyre, a member of one of the most prominent families in Derbyshire, stretching back to the time of William the Conqueror. His sons lived at houses surrounding the hall, one being Offerton Hall (passed on Walk 1). He would communicate with his sons by signalling to each of them from his home with a special semaphore code.

Go right along the road and take the first footpath left along the front of the hall to enter woodland. Proceed along the path through a gate crossing **Highlow Brook** via stile and bridge, and then going right to follow the Peak and Northern Footpath Society (PNFS) sign across a stile and up the track towards Abney. Keep on the track crossing a further stile to descend to **Stoke Ford**.

Go left and then left again following the wide footpath through a gate and a stile uphill until you reach a second PNFS sign. Follow its directions to Eyam, taking the central grassy path to the **triangulation pillar** on **Sir William Hill**. Go E at the pillar and follow the wall to a stone stile. Cross into Sir William Hill Road and take the stile immediately opposite, walking S until you reach a stone stile. Cross the stile and go left along the road then right through a gate to cross the fields along the public footpath, then go through a gate at the top corner woodland. Go into the woodland via the nearby gate on your right and follow the footpath down to the road passing the YHA hostel on your right. Turn right and follow the road back to **Eyam** car park.

WALK 8

Eyam Village

Start/Finish	Eyam SK 216 767
Distance	5.5 miles (9km)
Ascent/Descent	370m
Time	3hr
Terrain	Footpath, woodland, open fields, minor roads
Map	OS 1:25000 Explorer OL24 White Peak
Refreshments	Eyam
Parking	Eyam SK 216 767

A walk around Eyam gives a poignant perspective of the terrible events that befell the tiny community in 1665. The horror of what they experienced as the plague engulfed the village can only be surmised. As you walk around you can track the progress of the disease as it decimated the men, women and children. They made the courageous decision to seal themselves off from the outer world to prevent the deadly infection from spreading. At the visitor centre you can pick up a map of the village with all the plague information.

From **Eyam** car park turn left down Hawkhill Road towards the centre of Eyam. At the junction turn right and walk up **Town Head** to the junction with Tideswell Lane to view the old silk mill. Retrace your steps, stopping to look at Merrill Cottage on the way and West End Cottage, where nine people died of the plague. ▶

Merrill Cottage was home to Humphrey Merrill, the Eyam herbalist at the time of the plague.

The **bubonic plague** arrived in a bundle of cloth sent from London to the local tailor George Viccars. According to church records, 273 people lost their lives in little over a year. Around the village are information boards detailing the deaths in each household.

Take care on the slippery limestone in wet weather.

Continue into the centre of the village passing the village craft and information centre and turn right opposite the entrance to **Eyam Hall**. Walk down New Close then turn left into Dunlow Lane. Where the lane turns sharp right take the footpath on the left across fields following it to **Cucklett Delph**, where services were held during the plague. ◄

Each year on the last Sunday in August the plague is commemorated at **Cucklett Delf** as part of the ancient well dressing ceremony. The present

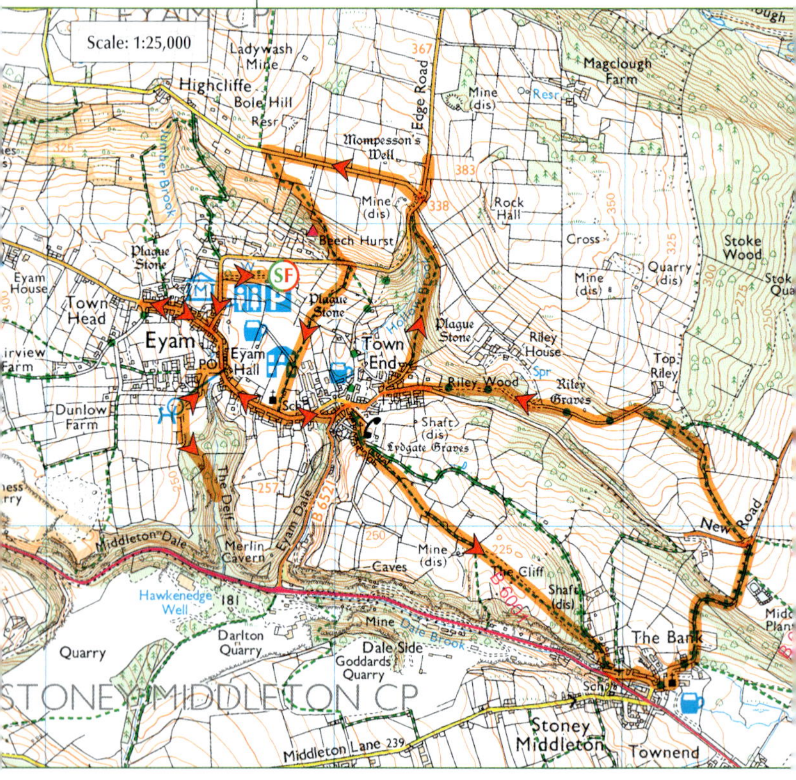

13th-century parish church is well worth visiting. There is a wonderful Saxon cross in the churchyard and inside are 16th-century murals on the clerestory walls. Outside, the grave of cricketer and umpire Harry Bagshawe finds him at the wicket.

Retrace your steps to visit **Eyam Hall** and walk down Church Street, paying attention to the plague cottages. Keep left where the road forks to arrive at The Square. Cross the **B6521** and walk up Lydgate viewing the **Lydgate plague graves** as you proceed along the ancient way from Eyam to Stoney Middleton. Where the road forks, take the right-hand fork to Stoney Middleton, passing the Boundary Stone, then drop down into **Stoney Middleton**. ▶

The Boundary Stone marked the boundary between Eyam village and Stoney Middleton and became a place where people outside the village would leave food during the plague.

The Boundary Stone

At the footpath junction with Mill Lane turn right and descend into the village. Where the road meets **The Bank** proceed straight ahead until the road turns sharp right. Here turn left onto The Nook and visit the unusual Octagonal Church. Carry on along the Nook to **New Road**. Go straight across and take the bridleway NW up through fields to woodland. Follow the track through the woods, bearing left where it meets another track to reach Riley Lane. Turn left here and walk along the lane passing the **Riley Graves** on your right.

Join the **B6521** and take the next road right, Riley Back Lane, then bearing right where it forks to ascend through trees to Edge Road. Turn right along the road and, just after a junction on the left, visit **Mompesson's Well**.

At **Mompesson's Well** money would be left soaked in vinegar to prevent infection for those delivering food and supplies to the villagers. This was one of several sites at the main entrances to the village. The well is named after the vicar who became the driving force, along with the Puritan Thomas Stanley, behind the decision to cut the village off from the outside world and thereby stop the spread of the plague. After an initial series of deaths in the autumn of 1665 the disease halted its progress for winter, only to begin anew the following year. It must have been a terrifying ordeal for the community, made all the more painful by having to bury their own.

Retrace your steps and follow Edge Road S to the previous junction then go right up the minor road until you reach a public footpath on the left. Go through a gate to cross the fields along the footpath, then through a second gate into a field at the top corner of woodland. Go into the woodland via the nearby gate on your right and follow the footpath down through the woods, passing the YHA hostel on your right until you reach Edge Road again. Cross diagonally left and take the right-hand of two footpaths to descend SW through fields to Eyam church. On exiting the churchyard turn right along Church Street and retrace your steps to **Eyam** car park.

WALK 9

Tideswell to Cressbrook

Start/Finish	Tideswell SK 152 757
Distance	6 miles (10km)
Ascent/Descent	285m
Time	3hr
Terrain	Minor country roads, open fields
Map	OS 1:25000 Explorer OL24
Refreshments	Tideswell
Parking	Tideswell SK 152 757

Tideswell, pronounced locally 'Tidsa', is a wonderful base for walking in the White Peak. This walk takes you to Water-cum-Jolly via the beautiful limestone dales of Tideswell and Cressbrook. The route is filled with wildflowers, butterflies and birds, with the added accompaniment of the River Wye. Litton Mill, now apartments, was once the epitome of a Victorian dark satanic mill in its treatment of orphan children, a wretched chapter in the county's history.

From **Tideswell church** head S down the **B6049**, bearing left at Fountain Square, then continue S along Gordon Road until the junction with Richard Lane. Here go right and then immediately left down a marked footpath, heading through a gate into woodland, eventually to exit via a second gate back onto the B6049. Turn right down the road and cross to enter the national park car park at the head of **Tideswell Dale**. Walk to the right of the amenity block through the gate and take the right-hand lower trail.

Where the trail divides take the right-hand fork over the small footbridge and then, a little further on, exit through a gate onto a minor road. Go left for a short distance then take the footpath rising on the left through woodland. Where the path meets the perimeter wall of the **Field Study Centre**, follow the path left around the

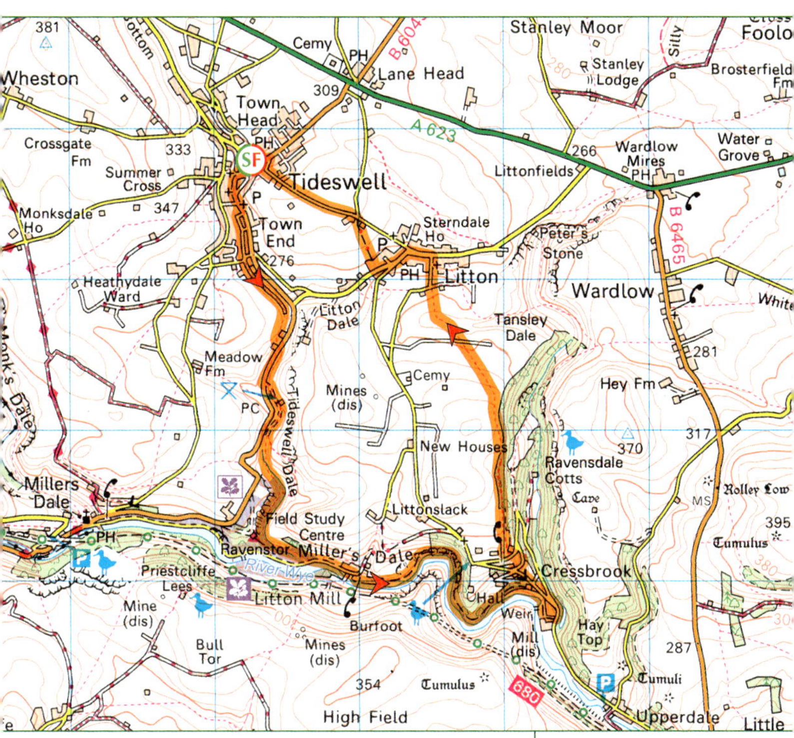

boundary and emerge onto a woodland track. Walk into
an open area facing the end of a row of cottages and bear
left. Walk along a narrow lane at the rear of the cottages
to a road junction then turn right down the minor road. At
Litton Mill go left through the gateway of the mill buildings and follow the road down past the cottages on the
left, turning right at the end to cross a footbridge to join
the trail to **Miller's Dale**.

Litton Mill casts a dark shadow over the Industrial
Revolution. Built by two local farmers wanting to
cash in on the new cotton trade, the mill lacked
both capital and a willing workforce. After several

years of struggle, the owners decided to use child labour as a major source of the workforce. They did not treat the children well and many died as a result of the poor working and living conditions. Eventually the mill passed through a succession of owners before falling into dereliction. Now it houses expensive apartments.

In times of flood it may be necessary to use the signposted diversion to arrive at Cressbrook.

The trail follows the **River Wye**, passing through the Cramside Wood Nature Reserve. ◄ If passable, continue down the trail until it crosses a weir at **Water-cum-Jolly** then turn left along a footpath in front of the renovated **Cressbrook Mill**.

Water-cum-Jolly has a beautiful setting. The idyllic pond and weir are surrounded by the limestone cliffs that are a favourite with rock athletes wanting to hone their craft.

At the road go left uphill to **Cressbrook Hall**. At the hall entrance, take the road opposite right and follow this around the hillside until you reach a rough lane on the left. Go up the lane and take the footpath immediately on the right between low walls. Cross an area of lawn to reach a minor road and follow a footpath to the gable end of a cottage. Turn right then right again by a low wall to a gate leading into a field. Go through the gate and take the footpath across several fields into woodland. Skirt the top of the woodland with the field boundaries on your left until you arrive at a stone stile on the left. Go over the stile then NW crossing six stiles or gates to enter a walled lane. Cross the lane keeping in a NW direction, passing the top of **Tansley Dale** and crossing three stiles before emerging onto a lane. Turn left towards the road and, at the junction, turn right and walk into **Litton**.

Go left along Church Lane, keeping left at the first fork in the road and right at the second. Then, 120 metres after passing Dale View, go right up Little Lane, first between houses then along a walled lane crossing open fields. Where it meets Church Lane go left and follow

CATHEDRAL OF THE PEAK

The church of St John the Baptist in Tideswell is known locally as the Cathedral of the Peak. It is a fitting accolade. The church is magnificent. Built during the years of the Black Death, construction continued unabated. As with many important buildings in the Peak, wool and the money it contributed to the economy funded much of the architecture we see around today. However, the 13th century was not without problems: monks from competing priories, battling for the control of Tideswell, were

The beautiful 'poppy heads' showing the stages of life from birth to death

not averse to the odd incident of sheep rustling and ransom. The church certainly has some fine features, the windows being some of the most imposing in Derbyshire. There are many monuments and effigies, along with brasses of Sir John Foljamb and also Bishop Robert Purseglove in a style of vestments from before the Reformation. Make sure you see the series of intricately carved misericords at the ends the pews.

the lane NW into Tideswell. Where Church Lane bends right, overlooking the church, take the footpath left and descend back into **Tideswell Village**.

WALK 10

Curbar to Gardom's Edge

Start/Finish	Curbar Gap SK 262 746
Distance	7.5 miles (12km)
Ascent/Descent	410m
Time	4.5hr
Terrain	Footpaths, tracks, some exposed edges
Map	OS 1:25000 Explorer OL24
Refreshments	Baslow
Parking	Curbar Gap SK 262 746

This short walk packs in so much it is one not to be ignored. There are fine gritstone edges to amble along, giving incredible views across the Peak District, and wonderful parkland and forests to stroll through at leisure. The walk is filled with curiosities from the Victorian age, as well as significant Neolithic archaeological remains in the form of rock cup and ring art. There is even a pub halfway around.

Baslow Moor may have cattle and sheep grazing upon it, and there will also be ground-nesting birds in season. At such times it is recommended that dogs be kept on a lead.

Take the western exit out of the car park at **Curbar Gap**, following the signpost for Baslow Edge. Cross the road and follow the footpath through the gate, then veer right to the viewpoint on **Baslow Edge**. ◄

Continue along the edge footpath until you meet the bridleway just S of a very large boulder on your left called the Eagle Stone.

The Eagle Stone has many bouldering routes whose names tend to the comedic, such as 'Where Beagles Dare', 'For a Few Beagles More' and 'Like a Beagle Over Troubled Water'.

Turn right and walk down the bridleway through the gate, walking onwards where the track becomes surfaced until you reach a tarmac road. Turn left at the small

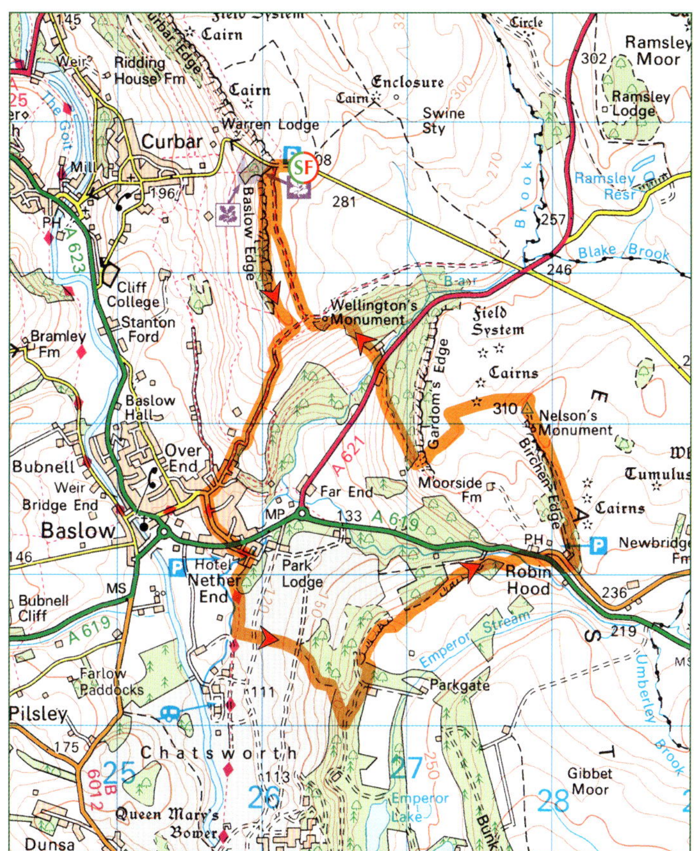

triangular green in **Baslow** and follow the road down then cross the **A619**. Walk straight ahead past the car park on your right, then turn right after the bridge and walk by thatched cottages on the left to go through a kissing gate leading into **Chatsworth Park**.

Immediately turn left following a fingerpost across the parkland and over two tracks. At the next junction follow the track opposite on the right of woodland to a gate giving access to the woods. Do not go through the gate but go right and follow the wall until you reach a stone stile. Go over the stile and follow the footpath up through woodland to a surfaced track. Turn left onto the concession footpath NE to Robin Hood, keeping on the track and ignoring any side junction until you reach a gate in a wall. Again, do not use the gate but go left then right over a high stone stile then along the footpath across fields and another stone stile. After crossing the next field take the wooden stile in the wall corner and follow the wall line through a squeeze stile left, then walk by the left-hand wall to cross a wooden stile. Take the footpath along Dobb Edge, keeping to the right for safety, and ascend the ladder stile over a tumbled wall. Go along the path through trees and shrubbery to a fingerpost, then downhill and cross a wooden footbridge spanning a brook. Ascend onto a road. Take great care when stepping out onto the **A619**. Cross the road and walk right along the pavement then bear left at the road junction to pass the **Robin Hood pub**.

After the pub and car park go left up the track and through the gate, then follow the footpath until it splits below **Birchen Edge**. Take the right-hand fork up onto the gritstone edge. Go left and follow the footpath to the **triangulation pillar** at the far end.

> **Birchen Edge** is a rather special place. There are numerous climbing routes along this gritstone edge but what really makes it unique are the wonderful views and the monument to Admiral Lord Nelson and three of his ships: *Victory*, *Defiance* and *Royal Soverin*. In summer it is a place to sit and enjoy the landscape as it slips from gritstone to limestone.

Descend from the edge via the footpath W of the pillar and carry straight on to the corner N of a wall. Take a bearing slightly SW (to grid reference SK 2728 7304) into the woodland in the W and, after 350 metres, arrive at the rock art stone with standing stone beyond. Regain the wall and continue SW along to a stone stile.

GARDOM'S EDGE

Gardom's Edge is possibly the only geological feature in the UK named after a blacksmith. Gardom was an expert in wrought ironwork, much of which is on show at Chatsworth. Gardom's Edge is an archaeologist's delight. Within a small space there are several items of interest. The most fascinating is the large flat stone with cup and ring marks. Found in the 1960s, the marks possibly date back to the Neolithic period or the Bronze Age. The stone is now protected to prevent further erosion. Nearby is a large standing stone, a 'menhir', and carved millstone. A little further afield can be found the remains of a round house and walled enclosure, signs that at a settlement was established here.

Cross the stile and, with the cairns known as the Three Men directly in front, turn left through a gap in the wall and follow the track down to meet a footpath running NE into woodland. Follow the path until you reach the **A621**, cross over and enter woodland opposite. Walk down the footpath through the woodland and cross over the packhorse bridge, then go left through a wooden gate and follow the steep path up through the woods. Where the path turns SW at the corner of a wall go right, directly N, and follow the guidepost up a very steep bank through trees to emerge by **Wellington's Monument**.

The author and search dog Scout at the cup and ring stone on Gardom's Edge

Wellington's Monument on Eaglestone Flat

Wellington's Monument looks across to Nelson's Monument. The former commemorates the victory at Waterloo by Wellington and his troops in 1815, while the latter celebrates the victory at Trafalgar in 1805. Nelson's Monument predates Wellington's by 56 years.

Go left then right along a wide track and pass the Eagle Stone encountered earlier on in the walk. Continue along the track until you reach the gate leading onto the road and the car park at **Curbar Gap**.

WALK 11
Calver to Hassop

Start/Finish	Sough Lane, Calver SK 239 747
Distance	7.75 miles (12.5km)
Ascent/Descent	315m
Time	4.5hr
Terrain	Minor country roads, footpaths, tracks
Map	OS 1:25000 Explorer OL24
Refreshments	Calver, Pilsley
Parking	Sough Lane, Calver SK 239 747

This gentle walk takes in some of the less-frequented villages on the boundary between the gritstone Dark Peak and limestone White Peak. The walk begins at Calver on Sough Lane and follows the River Derwent before branching off across the peat moorlands that dominate the Dark Peak, then returning to limestone country. This is a good walk for lovers of the wildflowers and butterflies that are bountiful on the limestone terrain.

From **Calver**, walk SE along Sough Lane until you come to Calver Cross at Folds Head. ▶ Turn left and walk along Main Street to the junction with the **A623**, then sharp right down a narrow lane leading to houses. Where the lane meets a minor road, go right then left to a passage between two fences. Follow the passage through a gate into a field and walk along the hedge line and, in the next field, along the banks of the River Derwent. Go through a gate and squeeze stile and take the footpath along the edge of woodland with a wall on your left. Pass through a squeeze stile and gate to continue along the path onto open ground. Cross the grass to go through another squeeze stile and bear diagonally right across a field towards a gate in the trees. Exit the field onto a road and turn left. After 380 metres, at **Bubnell**, take the minor road on the right following the footpath sign. Turn left down a track then

A sough is a drain from a lead mine. Mining was one of the industries that transformed the White Peak from a stock-farming landscape into an industrial one.

through a gate into a field. Head right and follow the wall line up the field and through a gate. Go diagonally left and through another gate to follow the wall on your left S until you reach a minor road. Go right, and then take the first footpath left over a stone stile and cross the field to a gate. Go through and continue across another field, diagonally right, to drop down to a wooden stile leading onto the **A619**. Cross the road and take the path opposite uphill and through two gates, then turn left to follow the wall across fields and out onto the road, then go right, into **Pilsley**.

At the first junction go straight on, W along High Street, passing the **Devonshire Arms** on the right. The road eventually becomes a lane leading to open country. At the end turn right, down the public bridleway until it reaches the **A619**. Walk right for 80 metres and then cross the road and take the farm gate along the track into woodland. Follow the path through the woods to emerge at a farm. Walk through the metal farm gate immediately in front of you and take the footpath down to the road. Cross the road and go right along the footpath to **Hassop** passing the entrance to **Hassop Hall**.

CHURCH OF ALL SAINTS

Hassop's neoclassical Church of All Saints is well worth exploring. Built by the prominent Derbyshire Eyre family, the Etruscan temple frontage forms an imposing entrance. Inside is a coved, coffered ceiling and, below, a secret tunnel that led to Hassop Hall. The church was part of the Hassop Estate, which stretches back to pre-Norman times when it was called Hetesope.

The estate has had a colourful past: one distant heiress was sold twice, each time at a profit, until she finally became betrothed to a son of the Plumpton family – and all before she was 11 months old. During the split from Rome, the Eyre family remained resolute in their Catholic faith, which made things extremely difficult. And in the Civil War, the estate became a Royalist stronghold and had to be bought back at enormous cost.

Turn left and walk up the road until it levels out by a green gate on your left. Take the footpath directly opposite, through the gate and across the field to go through a gap at the junction of three walls. Continue along the same line across the field to a road. Walk right, through **Rowland** and, as the road becomes a track on **Hassop Common**, go over two cattle grids then, where the track splits, take the left fork. Where it meets a walled lane by **Deep Rake Quarry** go right then immediately left through a gate into a field. Walk down the field diagonally left, then through a gate at the right of a barn and continue along the track. Where it meets a second track, go right then at the fork go left and cross a wooden stile. Follow the fence line to enter a walled lane via a farm gate. Walk down the lane passing a large dewpond on the left and, shortly after, going through a gate to open ground and exiting onto Hassop Road. Turn left and then right at the next junction to arrive back in Sough Lane, **Calver**.

WALK 12

Calver to Great Longstone

Start/Finish	Sough Lane, Calver SK 239 747
Distance	8 miles (13km)
Ascent/Descent	360m
Time	4.5hr
Terrain	Public footpaths across fields and well-made tracks
Map	OS 1:25000 OL24 or OS 1:50000 Landranger 110
Refreshments	Calver
Parking	Sough Lane, Calver SK 239 747

This short walk is a good introduction to the limestone area. Longstone Edge has spectacular views across the White Peak and down the Derwent Valley, with Chatsworth House holding centre court. From Longstone Edge the route crosses the final piece of heather moorland on the very cusp of both White and Dark Peak. Then it enters one of the famous Derbyshire dales: Coombs Dale, a narrow gorge carpeted with wildflowers and alive with butterflies.

Walk SE along Sough Lane from nearby **Calver** cross-roads. Stay on Sough Lane, which continues SW and becomes High Street, until it meets the **B6001** Hassop Road. Cross the road and go over the stile opposite into the field. Follow the footpath uphill to a stone track, turning right along the track and then shortly after left at the fingerpost, following its direction across a field to enter woodland by a tumbled-down wall. Follow the fence line on the left to a gate giving entrance to woodland. Go through the gate and along the woodland path. Exit through a second gate to cross a field and into a grassy lane via a gate, then onto a stone track. Turn right up the track and continue for 1 mile (1.6km) passing the protected ancient monument of a double dyke on your left.

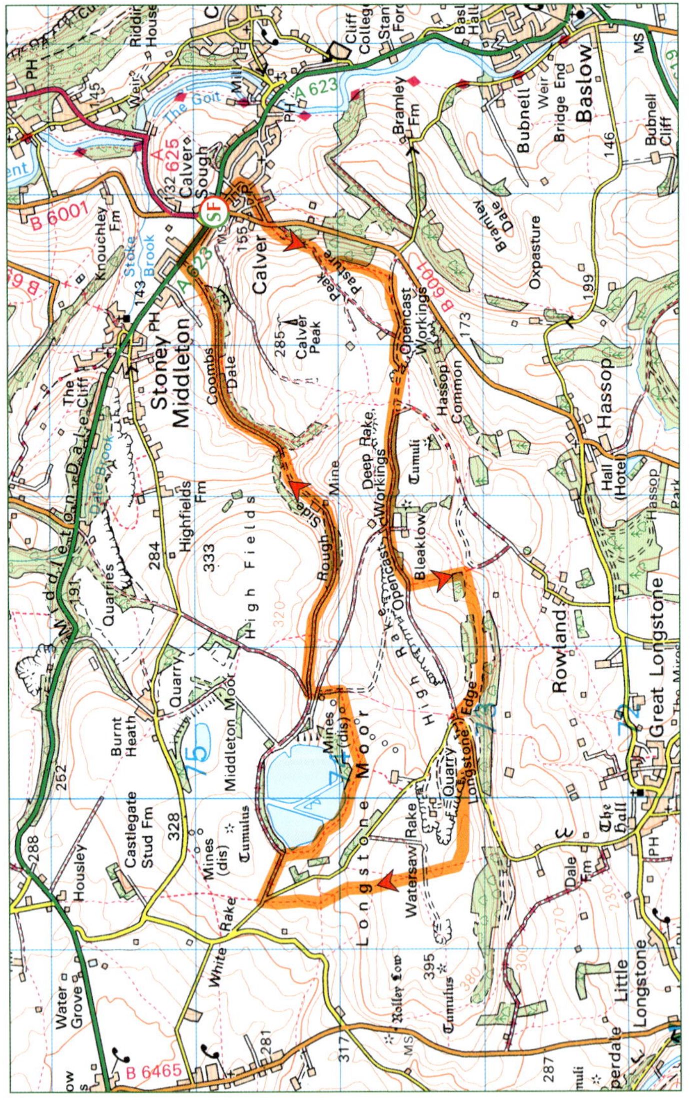
Riddings
House
PH
Weir
The Goit
Mill
A 623
Cliff
College
Stan
Ford
Bas
Hall
Baslow
MS
Bubnell
Weir
Bridge End
Bubnell
Cliff
146
B 6001
PH
A 625
Calver
Sough
Knouchley
Fm
Stoke Brook
143
A 623
Bramley
Fm
Calver
Oxpasture
Bramley Dale
199
Peak Pasture
Stoney
Middleton
Coombs Dale
Calver Peak
285
Opencast Workings
B 6001
173
Hassop
Common
Hassop
The
Cliff
Dale Brook
Highfields
Fm
333
High Fields
Deep Rake
Workings
Tumuli
Bleaklow
Hall
(Hotel)
Hassop
Park
284
320
Opencast
Rake
High Rake
Rowland
Great Longstone
191
Quarries
Quarry
Longstone Moor
High Rake
Longstone Edge
73
72
The
Mires
252
Burnt
Heath
Middleton Moor
75
Mines
(dis)
74
Watersaw Rake
Quarry
Longstone Edge
The Hall
PH
Dale
Fm
288
Housley
Castlegate
Stud Fm
328
Mines
(dis)
Tumulus
White Rake
395
Roller Low
Tumulus
287
Little
Longstone
281
B 6465
317
MS
270
300
380
230

The **double dyke earthwork** is one of only two in the White Peak area, located on the geological boundary between limestone and gritstone. It is a scheduled ancient monument and as such is protected by law. There are thought to be only 50 monuments of this kind in the whole country. Constructed across the ridgeway in the Dark Ages, archaeological evidence would support the theory that it was either defensive or marked the boundaries between two kingdoms: Pecsaetna, the ancient tribe of the Peak, and North Mercia.

At the end of the woodland where the track swings right by **High Rake Quarry** on the right-hand side, go left down a restricted byway. Take the second stile on the right, follow a footpath uphill then left along the track on **Longstone Edge**. Continue along the track for 800 metres, then cross the stile into a field and go diagonally left to a tarmac road. Cross the road and follow the footpath directly opposite over a stile and onto access land.

The view from **Longstone Edge** clearly shows the separation between the gritstone and peat of the Dark Peak to the north and the limestone pastures of the White Peak to the south. Looking out across Great Longstone, you can see successive enclosures. The long, narrow fields close to the centre of habitation are the oldest; then, moving out from the village, the fields become squarer and more regular; and finally, on the skyline, large areas of high common land are enclosed with long walls. This progression of Enclosure by Act of Parliament gradually removed land from the commoner and placed it into the hands of the land-owning families.

Follow the footpath with the fence on the right and views across the White Peak on the left, keeping to the fence as it turns right uphill. At the top of the hill go left along a track to a stile in a wall. Go over the stile and onto moorland. Walk along the footpath for 130 metres

There is a great deal of mining and quarrying activity in the White Peak. Never enter any workings and always be vigilant for traffic on nearby lanes.

Rosebay willowherb and ringlet butterfly (Aphantopus hyperantus)

then turn right at a small cairn and head out across **Longstone Moor** to a stile in a stone wall. Go over the stile and across fields to reach a road. Turn right and take the immediate left-hand fork along a track. Where the track turns sharp left by a dewpond, go right through a gate and follow the footpath around a small lake, sometimes dried up, to a stile in a wall. ◄

Cross the stile into the field and follow the wall line on your right across Blakeden Hollow. Where the wall turns sharp right, go NE diagonally across the field. Go through the gate and follow the footpath down, ignoring the sign for the bridleway on your right, to arrive at a second gate. Go through the gate to Black Harry Gate and take the right-hand lane, almost due E, to **Rough Side**. Follow the footpath, passing Sallet Hole Mine on the right and finally enter **Coombs Dale**.

Rough Side and Coombs Dale are perfect places for photographing **butterflies**. There is an abundance of the common rock rose and violets preferred by the brown argus and the dark green fritillary. Altogether you can spot in the region of 20 butterflies, including ringlet, small and large skippers, brimstone, common blue and small copper.

Proceed along Coombs Dale to emerge onto the **A623**, where you should turn right and follow the road back to **Calver** crossroads and the start of the walk.

WALK 13

Taddington to Monsal Dale

Start/Finish	Taddington SK 141 710
Distance	7 miles (11.5km)
Ascent/Descent	440m
Time	4hr
Terrain	Minor country roads, open fields, trail
Map	OS 1:25000 Explorer OL24
Refreshments	Taddington
Parking	Main Road, Taddington SK 141 710

The linear village of Taddington stands at 335 metres above sea level making it one of the highest in Derbyshire. The settlement is surrounded by evidence of both Celtic and medieval farming. The Five Wells Neolithic chambered cairn to the west of the village is worth inspection and provides a wonderful viewpoint across the White Peak. The walk takes you below the Headstone Viaduct at Monsal Dale, a sublime perspective from which to experience this magnificent structure.

From St Michael and All Angels Church in **Taddington**, walk E along Main Road until you reach a fork at Town End. Take the right-hand fork and at the first left-hand bend in the road, go right up a walled public footpath. Where the path forks, go left and follow the walled path to a T-junction. Go left and at a minor road left again, then right at the next road junction. Continue until the road stops in front of farm gates at **Taddington Field**. Go through the gate to your right then follow the footpath across the field as it drops down towards woodland. Go through the gate continue down the footpath following the signs for Monsal Dale. Emerge from the woodland via a stile then cross a second stile to enter open ground with short sections of limestone pavement showing. Continue along the path as it skirts the hillside, then go left at the signpost for Monsal Dale and walk along the path to White Lodge car park. Go N, straight across the car park, and exit onto the **A6**. Cross the road and go through the gap in the wall directly opposite, then bear diagonally left, cross a stream and go over a wooden stile. Follow the signpost for **Monsal Head** along the banks of the **River Wye** until you reach the impressive Headstone Viaduct.

HEADSTONE VIADUCT

The beautiful Headstone Viaduct sitting high above Monsal Dale is one of the most famous images of the Derbyshire Dales. Built in 1863 to take the rail line from Bakewell to Buxton, the viaduct is 91 metres long and 21 metres high, with each arch having a 15-metre span. The construction of the line caused great consternation in certain quarters due to the destruction of the beautiful dale. John Ruskin, for example, was vehemently opposed to the progress of the railways. Today the viaduct is seen as an engineering marvel and a thing of beauty that provides pleasure for people on foot, wheel and hoof.

The Headstone Viaduct. Note the steel bars across the arches to prevent people from bridge swinging

Go through the gate and under the arch of the viaduct and follow the river upstream. Just before the footpath crosses a footbridge, go sharp left back on yourself and take the rising footpath up to a gate and onto the **Monsal Trail**. Go right along the trail in the direction of Upperdale.

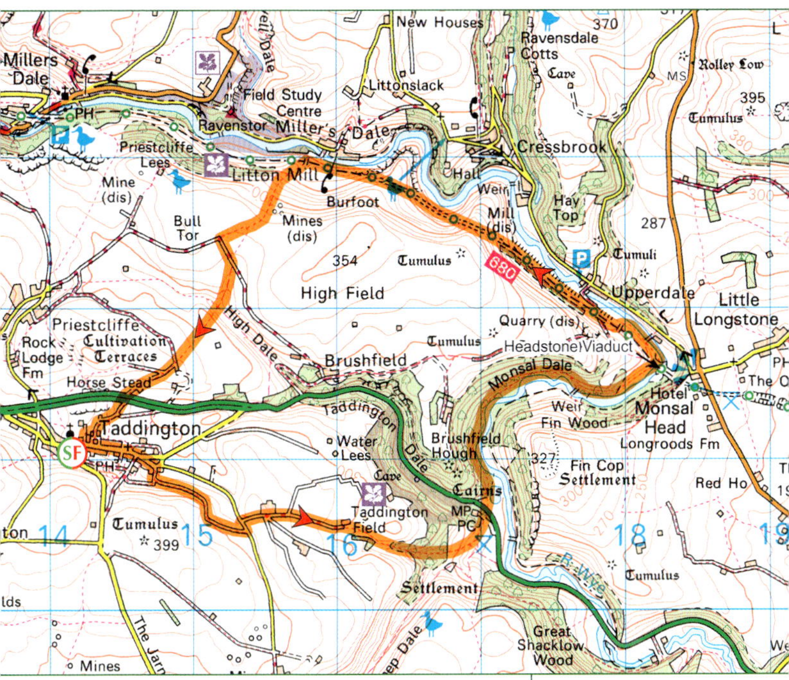

Shortly after passing through the second of the two tunnels, Litton Tunnel, go up the steps to the left of a railway bridge and, at the top, go through the gate and left into **Priestcliffe Lees Nature Reserve**. Walk up the steep hill aiming for the left-hand corner of the field, go over the stile and follow the wall line on your right until the footpath goes over a stile in that wall and takes you through a long, narrow field to deposit you onto a farm track. Go left down the track and take the footpath next right across fields to drop down into **High Dale**, then climb up the other side. Continue SW across fields until you enter a walled lane which you should follow SW until you meet the **A6** road. Cross the road and continue along a walled lane that delivers you once again onto Main Road in the centre of **Taddington**.

WALK 14

Chatsworth to Beeley

Start/Finish	Chatsworth House SK 260 703
Distance	7.75 miles (12.5km)
Ascent/Descent	250m
Time	4.5hr
Terrain	Minor country roads, footpaths, tracks
Map	OS 1:25000 Explorer OL24
Refreshments	Chatsworth, Beeley
Parking	Chatsworth car park

Chatsworth is one of Britain's great country houses. This relaxing walk from the house takes you through the woodlands surrounding the gardens and up onto the moor, then brings you back via one of the estate villages where there is a first-class pub. The return journey to the house is alongside the River Derwent, taking you through the landscape of Capability Brown, with some of the finest views of this superb stately home. There is no charge to walk in Chatsworth Park.

Each year Chatsworth Estate holds events ranging from art and music to show jumping and country pursuits. The Christmas period is always a special and magical time at Chatsworth.

From the stables at **Chatsworth House** walk NE along a tarmac drive until you reach the pedestrian entrance to Stand Wood on the right. Go through the iron gate and turn left up the tarmac trail to enter woodland. Bear left at the fork of two trails then go straight ahead, S, crossing over another trail until you come to a fork where you should go left.

Go around two hairpin bends as the trail zigzags up through the woodland. After the second hairpin, join the woodland trail on the left leading N and follow this trail to the **Hunting Tower.** ◄

Built for Bess of Hardwick, the Hunting Tower is a prominent feature looking over the landscape created by Capability Brown. The tower is now a holiday rental property.

CHATSWORTH ESTATE

From here you can enjoy fine views of Chatsworth house, gardens and park. Bess of Hardwick began construction of the house in the 16th century. The architectural style is a mixture of Italianate and English Baroque. The house contains many items of fine art from the world's most prestigious artists. One of the most striking works is the trompe l'oeil by Jan van der Vaart, a painting depicting the three-dimensional illusion of a violin and bow hanging on a door. The gardens and park owe much of their current form to the work of Lancelot 'Capability' Brown and Joseph Paxton, of Crystal Palace fame. Paxton created the Emperor Fountain for the planned visit of Tsar Nicholas I in 1844. For six months he worked round the clock to create the world's tallest fountain of water in honour of the Tsar who, in the end, never visited the house. Joseph Paxton also created the Great Conservatory at Chatsworth to grow exotic plants and fruit. It became the blueprint for the Great Exhibition Hall at Crystal Palace. Sadly, the conservatory was demolished in 1920 and now only the walls remain.

Retrace your steps and take the woodland trail next left from the tower, SE, following it around the **Emperor Lake** and later through the woods between Stan Wood and the lake in front of **Swiss Cottage** until you arrive at the tarmac drive leading to Park Farm. Go straight across and then over a stream and turn SE to a gate in a wall. Climb the high stone stile on the right and continue SE along a clear grass track until you reach a stone stile to the left of a farm gate. Go over the stile and across the track in front of you to enter **Hell Bank Plantation** via a gate directly opposite.

Just after entering the woods take the right-hand fork of the footpath and follow it down through the trees,

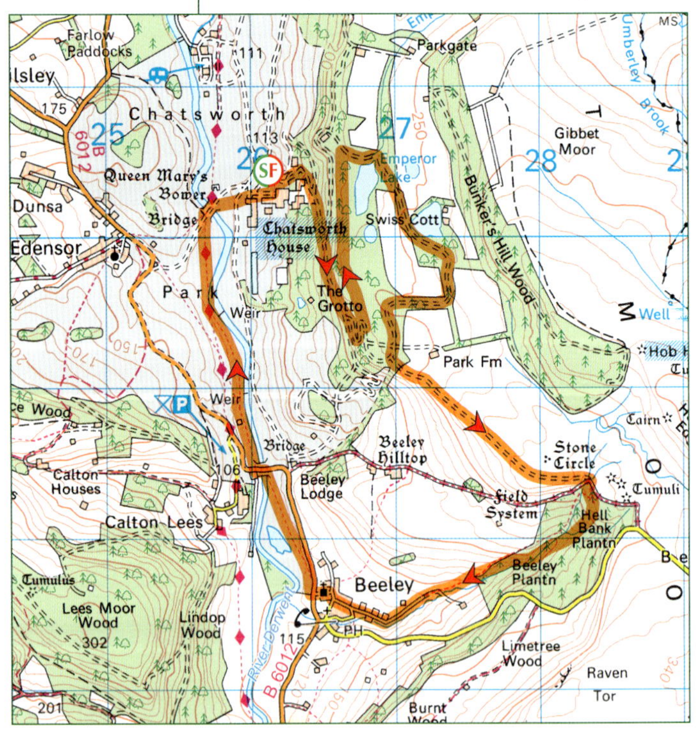

crossing a stream to eventually join a broader track that you should follow W, crossing a stream on the way and arriving at a stone wall. Go over the ladder stile and follow the wall line down through a gate to finally meet up with the road going into **Beeley**.

River Derwent, Chatsworth House and the Hunting Tower

Continue along the road, bearing right at a bench under a large tree, to the church. Turn left down the road, keeping the church on your right to the junction with the B6012. Cross the **B6012** and take the footpath opposite, across fields to the bridge over the **River Derwent**. Cross the bridge and take the footpath immediately on your right at the other side to walk along the bank of the river until you return to **Chatsworth House** at the next bridge.

WALK 15

Ashford in the Water to Monsal Head

Start/Finish	Ashford in the Water SK 194 696
Distance	7 miles (11.5km)
Ascent/Descent	460m
Time	4hr
Terrain	Minor country roads, public footpath
Map	OS 1:25000 Explorer OL24
Refreshments	Ashford in the Water, Monsal Head
Parking	Ashford in the Water, on-street parking

Starting at Ashford in the Water with its packhorse bridge and attached sheepfold, this walk follows the River Wye upstream to Monsal Head through some of the less-frequented Derbyshire dales. It delivers you to the foot of the Headstone Viaduct at Monsal Dale, a dramatic ending to the first half of the walk. From there a steep ascent onto the limestone plateau brings a gentle return to a welcome drink in the village.

The Sheepwash Bridge at Ashford in the Water

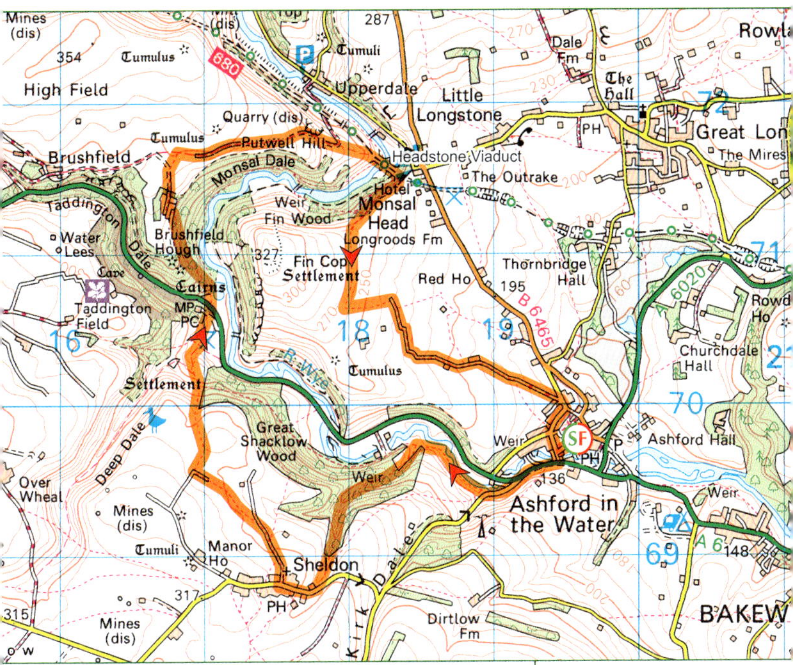

From Holy Trinity church, **Ashford in the Water**, walk SW along Fennel Street and, where it sweeps to the right, go left across the packhorse bridge onto the A6.

Attached to the bridge is an unusual **sheep wash**. At shearing time lambs were placed within the fold on one side of the river. The ewes were led into the water from the opposite side and as they swam across to get to their lambs, they were submerged beneath the water.

Go right, across the **A6**, then take the first minor road left, walking uphill until the road sweeps left. Go right through a gate and across the end of a field to a second gate. Pass through and walk along the riverside footpath then through a farm gate. Cross a field and, immediately after the next stile, turn left uphill to enter Little Shacklow Wood via a wooden stile.

Ascend the path through the woodland and, where it splits, take the left-hand fork uphill past the access to a cave. Emerge into pasture via a gate and continue up the field with the hedge on your right, eventually reaching the road into **Sheldon** via a wooden gate. Go right, into the village and, by the church noticeboard on Main Street, take the footpath right towards the church.

> **Sheldon** is a pre-Norman linear village high on the limestone plateau. Once the centre for lead mining and the quarrying of Ashford Black Marble, a shiny black limestone with fine grain, the village is now best known for its proximity to Magpie Mine.

From the church, follow Church Lane until it swings right then continue straight ahead down the walled lane, over a wooden stile until a prohibitive notice ahead bars the way. Follow the signpost on the left, going over the stone stile for White Lodge and Deep Dale. Cross a stone stile then cross five boundaries with stile or gate, heading NW to a second signpost. Go right, over a stone stile and along the line of the left-hand wall. Just after walking through a gateway, follow the fingerpost pointing left over a wall. Follow a second fingerpost diagonally right to the corner of **Great Shacklow Wood**. Go through a wooden gate and down a very steep hillside path. Midway down turn left along the track following the waymark signpost by the gate. Walk downhill and follow the fingerpost for White Lodge across **Deep Dale**. Go over the wooden stile then along the footpath following the fingerpost to a gate leading into White Lodge car park. Leave the car park and cross the **A6** to enter **Monsal Dale** via a gap in the wall directly opposite.

Bear left and follow the path across a stream. Go over the stile and proceed uphill following the fingerpost for Brushfield, up through woodland. At the top, go over the wall and follow the route along the farm track. Bear diagonally left at the fingerpost then take the footpath left between farm buildings. At the junction with another farm lane, go right. Continue up the wide farm lane at **Brushfield Hough**. Follow the lane to the signpost for Upperdale and turn E following a wall on your right through two farm gates. Where the track turns sharp left, descend the walled green lane straight ahead to a gate that decants you onto the **Headstone Viaduct** across Monsal Dale.

Cross the viaduct and, just before the Headstone Tunnel, take the footpath left up the steep hillside to reach **Monsal Head**. ▶ Do not go onto the road but follow the footpath right along the top of the steep hillside and, where it forks, take the left-hand path uphill, then through a gate and up steps. At the top turn left through a gate to enter a walled lane heading S. Alternatively, take the footpath to the right as you ascend the steps. The footpath takes you W along the escarpment above Monsal Dale to view the site of **Fin Cop fort and settlement**. The site is on private land with no access, so retrace your route to the walled lane to continue with the walk.

The Headstone Tunnel is 487 metres long.

FIN COP

The settlement at Fin Cop stretches back to Mesolithic times; flint and shards from the period have been found at the site. This would make it one of the first places in the White Peak to see a human hand. The position of the settlement gave it good protection from the steep slopes north and west, but the southern and eastern boundaries needed significant protection. The remains of ditches and bank suggest that, during several periods of occupation through to the Iron Age, defences were constantly being improved. During recent excavations the skeleton of a woman was found in one ditch. It was ascertained from the way the body was positioned that this was not a burial site. Upon further investigation the bones of a baby were also found within the remains, suggesting the woman was either pregnant or the baby had been thrown into the ditch alongside the female body. The following year excavations uncovered the remains of eight more bodies, in all two women, a young man, two children and four babies. Destruction of ramparts and the bodies suggest that the fort came to a violent end somewhere around 400BC.

Ashford in the Water

Pass through four farm gates to emerge onto a field by a large dewpond. Shortly after, turn left down a fenced and walled footpath. At the bottom turn right through a gate to continue along a walled lane that emerges onto a minor road. Turn right and follow the road downhill into **Ashford in the Water**.

WALK 16

Bakewell to Chatsworth

Start/Finish	Bakewell SK 218 685
Distance	9.5 miles (15.5km)
Ascent/Descent	340m
Time	5hr
Terrain	Minor country roads, public footpath and trail
Map	OS 1:25000 Explorer OL24
Refreshments	Bakewell
Parking	Bakewell car park SK 221 686

This is a walk from the Peak District's great market town to one of the country's great stately homes, returning through the estate of the medieval Haddon Hall. The walk gives fine views across the landscape of Capability Brown and Joseph Paxton as it winds its way through the Chatsworth Estate. Film and television stars can often be seen in some period drama at Haddon Hall. This is a minor grand tour of privilege.

From the national park information centre in **Bakewell**, walk NE along Bridge Street over the packhorse bridge, then take Coombs Road on the right. When you reach The Outrake, go left through the metal gate and ascend to a gate leading into a field. Go through and follow the right-hand wall over a wooden stile and across the bridge spanning the **Monsal Trail**. Go through a gate and follow the footpath diagonally right across a golf course to woodland. Follow the steep path generally E as it zig-zags its way up through the trees. Cross a stream half-way up then, on reaching the top, go through a gate in a wall onto **Calton Pastures**. Head for the right of a copse and continue E through two gates and a stile. After the stile, bear NE to meet a track running up from **Calton Houses**. Go left along the track and through a farm gate into woodland and follow a walled track down to a high

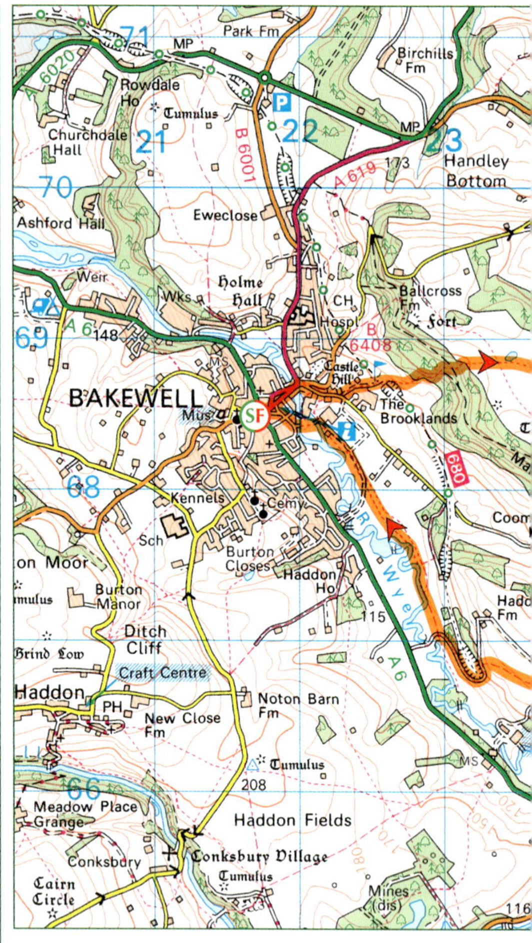

stone stile into **Chatsworth Park**. Follow the footpath down through the parkland NNE passing between two copses. Aim towards the boundary wall of **Edensor** and go through a kissing gate and down stone steps at the end of the short path to enter the village.

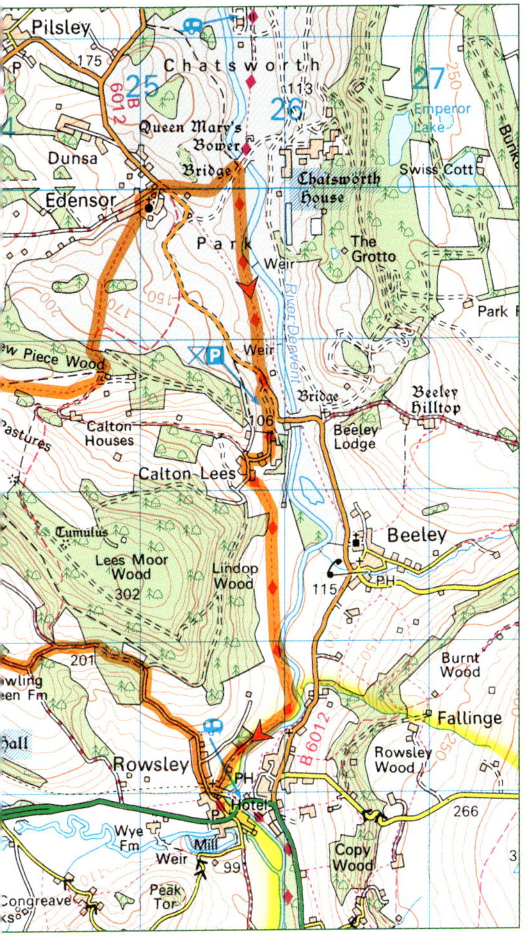

Turn right to exit the village via the kissing gate and cross the **B6012** then follow the footpath to **Chatsworth House**.

Just before you cross the bridge to the house, turn right and follow the River Derwent S to the B6012. Cross

EDENSOR

Edensor, pronounced 'Ensor', was moved out of sight of Chatsworth House in the middle of the 19th century. The planning of the new village was overseen by Joseph Paxton, and many of the buildings are listed.

The village church is well worth a visit. The pulpit and font are made from Ashford Black Marble. Paxton, head gardener of the Chatsworth Estate and designer of the Crystal Palace in London, is buried in the village churchyard, which is the final resting place of the Dukes of Devonshire. Deborah, one of the famous Mitford sisters, who later became the Duchess of Devonshire, is buried here. Next to her lies Kathleen Kennedy (sister of John Fitzgerald Kennedy), who had married the Marquess of Hartington (son of the 10th Duke of Devonshire).

The Chatsworth Estate village of Edensor has some beautiful houses

the road and enter the garden centre car park via the gate. Keep to the right of the garden centre entrance and walk along the road into **Calton Lees**. At the fork in the road bear left and then, as the road sweeps sharp right, just after a George VI letterbox, take the stile and footpath straight ahead into a field. Turn S along the Derwent

Valley Heritage Way across farmland to a ladder stile. Go over the stile and continue S crossing two more stiles to reach a gate. Go through the gate and along a short lane hedged on both sides, then through another gate onto pasture. Cross the grass and go through the gate into a lane running parallel with the **River Derwent** on your left.

Follow the lane and take the footpath right through a gate into the churchyard at **Rowsley**. ▶

Inside is a fine memorial to Lady John Manners (above), wife of the Seventh Duke of Rutland. It is carved in white statuary, the most precious marble in the world.

Exit the churchyard by the church gate and go right up the road until it becomes a lane. Continue along the lane until it meets the junction with a track running down to Coombs Farm. Turn left then at the next junction bear right, walking until the track turns sharp right. Follow the fingerpost along the footpath straight ahead and down a narrow lane to a gate. Go through the gate and cross a field, keeping metal railings on the left, then go through another gate to emerge onto a tarmac lane. Turn left along the lane passing a blocked-up railway tunnel entrance to the right.

The **Haddon Hall tunnel** was constructed to hide the Midland Railway line from Bakewell to Buxton from the Dukes of Rutland who resided at Haddon Hall. The Monsal Trail now runs along the former track bed and there are hopes to open up this tunnel and extend the trail further south down the Derwent Valley.

Continue along the minor road until it sweeps left just before reaching the **River Wye**. Follow the footpath right along the river, passing through a gate, until you reach the second of two footbridges crossing the River Wye. Cross the bridge and walk back into the town centre of **Bakewell**.

WALK 17

Bakewell to Monsal Head

Start/Finish	Bakewell SK 218 685
Distance	8.5 miles (14km)
Ascent/Descent	280m
Time	4.5hr
Terrain	Minor country roads, footpaths and trail
Map	OS 1:25000 Explorer OL24
Refreshments	Bakewell
Parking	Bakewell car park SK 221 686

This walk explores the traditional sheep-farming land of the White Peak. The church at Great Longstone is well worth viewing. If you time the seasons correctly, you may also come across the ancient practice of 'well dressing', carried out in many of the White Peak villages. Perhaps the highlight of the walk is the sight of the Headstone Viaduct spanning Monsal Dale from Monsal Head. This magnificent structure carried the Bakewell to Buxton railway line.

From the national park information centre in **Bakewell**, walk NE along Bridge Street over the packhorse bridge then, at the other side, take the footpath left through the meadow called Scott's Garden. Follow the well-defined path through two gates, walking upstream of the **River Wye** to emerge onto a road via a final gate. Go left and walk to the start of a second packhorse bridge. ▶

Do not cross the bridge but take the road on the right, up a lane between houses, passing on the left the home of Richard Arkwright Junior, a financier and son of Richard Arkwright who founded Cromford Mill. As you reach the rear of **Holme Hall** on your right, keep on the lane immediately to the left and continue uphill, eventually going

There are several packhorse bridges spanning the River Wye. The one near Holme Hall dates from 1664. The triangular pedestrian retreats are known as 'quoins'.

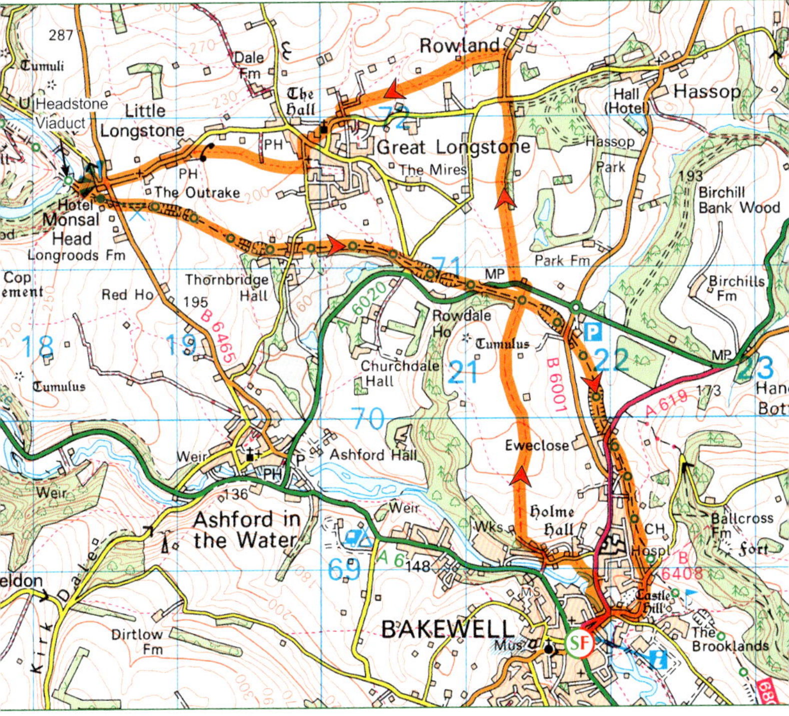

through a farm gate onto pasture. Follow the signposted footpath N, passing a dewpond on the left then reaching a gate into a walled lane. Proceed along the walled lane, passing through five farm gates and finally a pedestrian gate that leads you onto the **Monsal Trail**. Cross the trail and go through the gate opposite, then along the field and out via a farm gate onto a road with a Swiss cottage-style house opposite. Go left and cross the road at the bend, then take the footpath right over the stone stile and up the field heading to the left-hand edge of the tree plantation. Follow the line of the plantation boundary wall through four stiles onto a lane. Do not enter the lane but take the footpath immediately on the right that runs parallel to emerge on a road by some large gates.

Go left and then right at the next junction towards the village of **Rowland**. As you enter the village go past the first dwelling on the right. At the second house take the footpath immediately opposite on the left. Go through the stile and gate and cross the field heading W. Go through a second gate and aim for the left corner of a solitary barn. Cross a concrete track via stiles to reach the barn. Follow the footpath SW across several fields and over four stiles to arrive at Hardrake Lane. Continue over a stone stile opposite and walk SW to two stiles, one on either side of another concrete track. Cross over via the stiles and, in the same direction, walk over the fields using two more stiles to enter a narrow, walled lane. At the end, go left to the junction with the main road running into **Great Longstone**. Go right along the road then, at the cemetery, take the concession footpath to the church. After visiting the church, regain the road and walk down to the centre of the village.

The ancient practice of **well dressing** within Derbyshire villages may have originated as a pagan custom of offering thanks for the constant supply of life-giving waters from the local wells and springs. Each year a new theme is chosen by the villages, and the elaborate dressing of the boards with flower petals is often carried out in secret.

Go right, up the village street and, at the stone cross, take Station Road on the left. After passing the school, take the footpath opposite on the right through a squeeze stile. Follow the footpath generally W through three stiles to a walled lane. Cross the lane and continue W through another squeeze stile across fields to a narrow plantation. Go through the plantation using the gates then cross a field diagonally right, emerging through a gate onto the road at **Little Longstone**. Go left along the road to Monsal Head Hotel. At the junction bear right then left to arrive at **Monsal Head**.

Go through the gap in the wall and follow the footpath downhill, bearing left where the path forks to eventually arrive on the **Monsal Trail** at the Headstone Tunnel. ▶

Go left through the tunnel and follow the trail along for 3.2 miles (5.2km). At **Bakewell Station** leave the trail on the right and walk through the old station car park. Go left along the road to join the **B6048** at Castle Hill. Turn right and walk down the road back into **Bakewell**.

Four tunnels, illuminated during daylight hours, are now open along the trail. The general etiquette is to keep to the left-hand side.

Illuminated tunnel along the Monsal Trail

WALK 18

Bakewell to Over Haddon

Start/Finish	Bakewell SK 218 685
Distance	7.5 miles (12km)
Ascent/Descent	290m
Time	4.5hr
Terrain	Minor country roads, footpaths
Map	OS 1:25000 Explorer OL24
Refreshments	Bakewell
Parking	Bakewell car park SK 221 686

It is well worth visiting the thriving market town of Bakewell on a Monday, market day, when it is in full bustle. The walk visits several small hamlets inhabited since medieval times and with much evidence of their feudal past. The walk culminates in a descent to Haddon Hall, one of the great country houses in the area and virtually untouched for centuries. The return to Bakewell alongside the River Wye ends this peaceful walk.

From the national park information centre in **Bakewell**, walk SW along Bridge Street and at the roundabout go straight on, up the **B5055**, keeping the Rutland Arms Hotel on your right. Take the third junction left, Yeld Road, and shortly after, immediately at the end of a house on the right, go up steps. At the top, walk straight on between bungalows then along a tarmac footpath leading to a road. Walk SW, first along the road then a footpath, to exit onto a main road opposite a **school**. Cross the road and take the footpath to the right of the school across a field to a stile. Go over the stile and follow the right-hand hedge line to the next boundary then turn left and follow the wall down across fields.

Go through two gates close together and follow the right-hand field boundary up **Ditch Cliff** to a gate and stile. Cross the wall and bear left uphill to cross a wooden stile immediately in front of a squeeze stile. Turn left and walk onto the Bakewell Road leading to **Over Haddon**. ▶ Follow the road down to the centre of the village where it becomes Main Street as it sweeps right.

Maurice Oldfield, a son of Over Haddon village and former head of MI6, was said to have been the inspiration for George Smiley in John le Carré's novel *Tinker Tailor Soldier Spy*. He is buried in the village churchyard.

Over Haddon is mentioned in the Doomsday Book. Surrounding the village, you can see the open medieval field system, with its long, narrow fields and undulating drystone walls.

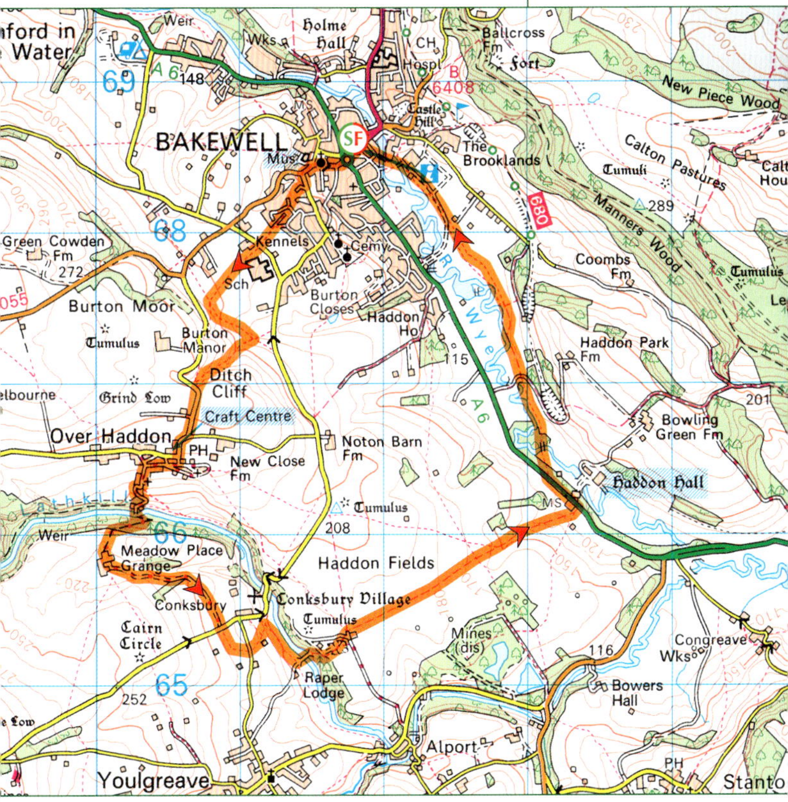

The medieval open field system around Over Haddon

Walk down Dale Road and cross the clapper bridge over the **River Lathkill**. Take the track up the hillside initially E then W to emerge out of the trees at a farm gate. Go through the gate and walk across the field diagonally left to reach **Meadow Place Grange**. Go into the farmyard and follow the farm track past the house, then E away from the farm.

Continue on the track passing the site of the medieval village of **Conksbury** and cross the road, then go through the squeeze stile opposite. Cross the field to a second stile and head diagonally left to exit by a squeeze stile onto a road. Go left along the road and take the first footpath right through a gate down to woodland. Follow the footpath SE through the woodland, going over a stile and through a gate to arrive at **Raper Lodge**. Go left down the lane and cross the **River Lathkill** by the weir, then walk uphill to a farm gate leading onto **Haddon Fields**.

Go through the gate and follow the bridleway, keeping to the left of the large tree plantation, then go through a second gate near a barn and follow the wall line NE to descend to **Haddon Hall** on the A6.

> Parts of **Haddon Hall** date from the 12th century. It has been in the Manners family for many generations. Historian Nikolaus Pevsner said the house was 'the English castle par excellence'. It has featured in many period dramas of both film and television. The Long Gallery and the Chapel are particularly fine.

Cross the **A6** to enter Haddon Hall or walk left along the road to take the footpath on the right through the hedge. Follow this path alongside the **River Wye** until you come to a minor road. Go right then take the footpath next left and keep following the river upstream until you reach the second of two footbridges that will take you back into the centre of **Bakewell**.

Haddon Hall

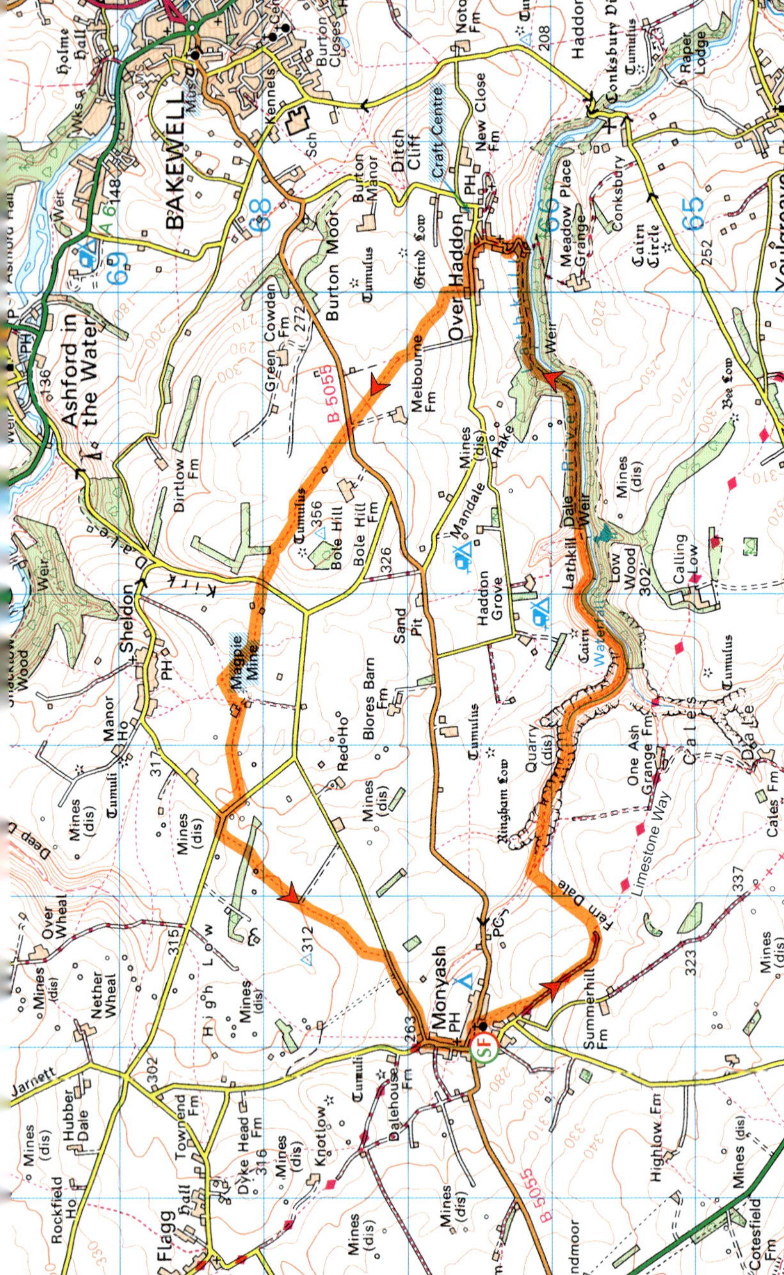

Holme Hall
Holme Hall Wks
BAKEWELL
Mus
Kennels
Sch
Cem
Burton Closes
Burton Manor
Burton Closes Ho
Ditch Cliff
Craft Centre
PH
New Close Fm
Noton Fm
208
Haddon
Haddon Lodge
Raper Lodge
Conksbury Br
Conksbury
Cairn Circle
Youlgreave
252
65
66
68
69
Ashford in the Water
PH
136
148
A 6
Weir
Weir
Over Haddon
Grind Low
Tumulus
Burton Moor
Green Cowden Fm
272
270
290
300
B 5055
Melbourne Fm
Weir
Meadow Place Grange
Bee Low
Dirtlow Fm
280
200
Tumulus
356
Bole Hill
Bole Hill Fm
326
Mines (dis)
Mandale Rake
Mines (dis)
Lathkill Dale
Low Wood
302
Mines (dis)
310
320
Calling Low
Sheldon
PH
Kirk Dale
Deep Dale
Slidderow Wood
Weir
Manor Ho
Magpie Mine
Red Ho
Blores Barn Fm
Sand Pit
Haddon Grove
Cairn
Waterfall
Tumulus
317
Tumuli
Mines (dis)
Mines (dis)
Mines (dis)
Tumulus
Ringham Low
Quarry (dis)
One Ash Grange Fm
Cales Fm
Cales Dale
337
Over Wheal
Nether Wheal
315
High Low
Mines (dis)
312
Monyash
PG
Limestone Way
Fern Dale
323
Mines (dis)
302
Jarnett
Hubber Dale
Townend Fm
Dyke Head Fm
316
Mines (dis)
Knotlow
Dalehouse Fm
Tumuli
263
PH
SF
Summerhill Fm
Highlow Fm
374
Rockfield Ho
Flagg Hall
Flagg
Mines (dis)
Mines (dis)
Endmoor Fm
B 5055
Cotesfield Fm
330
340
300
280

WALK 19
Monyash to Sheldon

Start/Finish	Monyash SK 150 665
Distance	8.75 miles (14km)
Ascent/Descent	330m
Time	4.5hr
Terrain	Minor country roads, open fields, trail
Map	OS 1:25000 Explorer OL24
Refreshments	Monyash
Parking	Church St, Monyash. SK 149 666

Monyash is a lovely White Peak village with an interesting church and popular pub and café. It makes a good base for exploring the area. Lathkill Dale, a long sinewy ravine hewn by the crystal-clear River Lathkill, is full of interest for naturalists and geologists. The highlight of the walk is Magpie Mine, whose winding gear and engine house strike an imposing presence on the landscape.

Starting from the ancient market cross on **Monyash** village green, walk SE down Church Street and enter St Leonard's churchyard. ▶

Follow the footpath to the right of the church and continue down a short lane to emerge onto Rakes Road. Turn left and follow the road to a sharp right-hand bend. Carry straight on along an unmade lane with a sign confirming this is the **Limestone Way**. Follow the walled lane to a gate leading onto pasture at the head of **Fern Dale**. Turn NE down Fern Dale until you reach the path at the bottom. Turn right and enter the steep-sided limestone gorge through a gate, maintaining a SE direction along the floor of the gorge until you meet the **River Lathkill** as you walk through a gate.

Follow the river downstream until the public footpath ends at a gate. Go through the gate and enter the **Lathkill Dale Nature Reserve**.

The church contains many local artefacts from village life and is well worth exploring.

The **River Lathkill** is unusual in that its source moves depending on the weather. In high rainfall the river emerges from Lathkill Head Cave, whereas in dry periods it surfaces via springs lower down the dale. This is due to the limestone absorbing the water down into its many cave systems. Look out for, but do not pick, the rare Jacob's ladder (*Polemonium caeruleum*) on the right-hand slopes. You may see dippers and brown trout in the river, and buzzards soaring above. Fossils are visible on the limestone outcrops but please do not try and remove any.

Continue along the dale floor, walking through a gate onto the concession path E of the **weir**. Walk over the footbridge and pass Bateman's House on your right.

Bateman's House was built to hide the workings of a winching machine used in the construction and maintenance of a Dakeyne's disc pump that sat in the lead mine directly below the building. At the rear of the house visitors can descend a shaft that was used to access the main mine shaft.

Carry on along the concession path, passing the Mandale Engine House on the left, until you arrive at a tarmac road. Go left up the hill into **Over Haddon** and past the church, keeping left where the road forks to reach Monyash Road. Walk left along the road for 250 metres until you reach a footpath on the right just before a derelict barn. Go over the stone stile and walk N up the field. Then, at the next stone stile, strike NW across five stiles to reach the **B5055**. Go straight across the road and over the stone stile to follow the fingerpost NW across four stiles to a wooden stile leading onto an open area bordered by tall trees. Cross the open field then go over a stone stile into a narrow, wooded copse. Turn immediately left and go over a wooden stile then walk NW downhill to a road. On the skyline you will see the remains of **Magpie Mine**. Cross the road and go through the gate to follow the footpath uphill to arrive at the mine.

MAGPIE MINE

Magpie Mine was one of the last working lead mines in Derbyshire. The atmospheric site contains the remains of a Cornish engine house and chimney, a horse-gin winding gear and associated buildings. The mine sat on one of the most lucrative lead veins in the country and bitter disputes between neighbouring mines were frequent, due to the proximity of the lead veins. In 1833 miners from Magpie lit a fire underground in an attempt to prevent workers from exploiting the lead vein of a competing mine. Three people died, but the Magpie miners were acquitted of murder, much to the anger of the dead workers' families. One of the widows placed a curse on the mine and all who worked there. From that point it is said the mine ceased to prosper. Mining operations stopped altogether in the 1950s and access into the mine is no longer possible.

From the mine, take the footpath due W through a gate crossing two further stiles to reach a minor road. Turn right along the road and follow it past the junction on the right. Take the next footpath on the left through a gate and cross the field to a small wooded copse. Pass through the trees using the stiles then follow five stiles and gates SW to emerge onto Horse Lane. Turn right and follow the road back into **Monyash**.

Magpie Mine can be an imposing site

WALK 20

Rowsley to Birchover

Start/Finish	Rowsley SK 256 658
Distance	9 miles (14.5km)
Ascent/Descent	300m
Time	4.5hr
Terrain	Minor country roads, open fields, trail
Map	OS 1:25000 Explorer OL24
Refreshments	Rowsley, Birchover
Parking	Rowsley SK 256 658

The highlight of this walk has to be Stanton Moor and the historical features that will be of interest to any avid collector of outdoor folklore. The Nine Ladies is probably the most popular stone circle in the whole of the Peak District. The walk is full of cairns, ancient ruins and boulders that were used to test a young man's suitability for marriage. There is a wealth of natural history to be enjoyed, with wildflowers and butterflies in abundance.

Stanton Woodhouse Farm

From **Rowsley** Old Station School, walk S and where the road turns right carry straight on along a tarmac lane for 1 mile (1.5km) until it reaches **Stanton Woodhouse**.

    Where the lane turns sharp right towards the farmhouse, go straight ahead through a farm gate. Follow the grass track initially S then SW up towards a wood on the skyline. Go through a metal gate and continue along the footpath until you reach a road. Walk right, up the road

150 metres, then take the footpath, left, that ascends into woodland.

Follow the footpath around the ruined buildings of the quarry and continue along the path rising through the woods. Eventually the path meets a wall separating the woods from fields. Turn left and follow the wall then fence until you come to a gate leading onto **Stanton Moor**. Go through the gate and continue straight ahead to the **Nine Ladies Stone Circle**.

STANTON MOOR

Nine Ladies Stone Circle, Stanton Moor

There are four stone circles on Stanton Moor. The Nine Ladies is the best known and the easiest to find. Dating back to the Bronze Age, the circle has connections with a nearby urn field where the remains of cremated bodies were placed. It is said that the stones were originally ladies who were turned to stone for dancing on a Sunday, and that the King Stone, situated outside the circle, was their fiddler. The Nine Ladies is still a place of worship and reverence today, with ceremonies taking place at both the winter and summer solstice. Dotted around the moor are several large boulders that provide tests of skill and strength for today's agile boulderers. The Cork Stone is the best example. Myth has it that a young man had to climb the stone for the right to ask a girl to marry him. It seems to be quite a common myth around this type of boulder, and it may bear some truth.

Go left at the circle and follow the track to the **Tower**. ▶ Then eventually bear right to arrive at the **Cork Stone**. Proceed past the stone and descend to a gate leading onto a road. Go left along the road then turn right into the car park opposite the quarry of Birchover Stone Ltd. Take the footpath on the far side of the car park down into woodland. Emerge onto The Mires road opposite the Druid Inn. If you have time, visit Rowter Rocks to the west of the village and explore the rock art, caves and features hewn by hand in the 17th century.

The tall, stone tower was erected to commemorate the Reform Act of 1832 and is known as The Earl Grey tower. It is an excellent spot for a brew.

Go left and follow the road through the village, then just after the pinfold, take the footpath right between two houses. Follow the footpath through the gate and around the barn then into open fields, keeping to the footpath signs through three stiles or gates to arrive at a gate and a stone stile. Go through and turn immediately right to follow the field boundary down to exit via a squeeze stile into a walled lane. Turn left and follow Clough Lane, keeping on the track where it enters woodland until it becomes the tarmac Oldfield Lane. Follow the lane downhill past a factory until it ends at a junction.

Turn right and continue down the hill to **Darley Bridge**. Take care of traffic. At the next junction turn left and follow the pavement on Main Road across the bridge to the entrance of the cricket ground. Go through the entrance and follow the **Derwent Valley Heritage Way** through three gates and across fields to **Churchtown**, eventually emerging onto the road by the church.

The churchyard at **St Helen's Church** is well worth visiting. Note the stone steps outside by the road, used for mounting a horse. Inside the grounds is a yew tree, said to be over 2000 years old. In the porch of the church are several intricately carved Saxon coffin lids, while inside the church are Norman and Jacobean fonts and a stained-glass window by Burne-Jones.

Walk past the church on the opposite side of the road then cross to bear left at the fork. Follow the Derwent

Saxon stone carving at St Helen's Church

Valley Heritage Trail through the gates to Abbey Farm. Go past the farm building and continue, crossing fields via five stiles, generally NW, to find yourself on a wide gravel track that delivers you to the Peak Railway, **Rowsley South Station**.

Follow the concession footpath past a small industrial estate. Where the gravel track ends at a roundabout, take the signposted footpath left into woodland and follow this as it winds its way N along the banks of the **River Derwent**, until you reach a car park. Bear right out of the car park, and then turn left down the road to the next junction. Turn left at the junction and, just after the pedestrian crossing, turn left again into Old Station Road.

Robin Hood's Stride (Walk 22)

INTRODUCTION

This is the pure White Peak: limestone gorges filled with a huge variety of wildlife and the famous trout streams of clear, cool water. The walking is a pastoral delight, crossing vivid green fields dotted with sheep; sparrow hawks quartering the land from above gives a sense of gentle calm. Take your time walking and savour the experience.

The history of this land stretches back a long way. There's evidence of human activity in the ancient burial chambers, such as the ones at Minninglow, or look out for fossils in the limestone around Thorpe Cloud. There are too many beautiful churches to mention, often with Norman origins, but make sure you visit the one in the tiny village of Thorpe for an insight into life in medieval times.

The landscape has also been subject to many of the major social developments in the country's history. Around Tissington, for example, you can see evidence of the feudal system in the ridge and furrow field ploughing, which was used to provide food for the lord of the manor and his subjects.

The many farms that carry the name 'grange' in their title signal land ownership by the monasteries and the change to the sheep-based economy that brought wealth to the area and helped build some of the great churches.

Towards the end of the Middle Ages the tradition of 'well dressing' became established and this is now a major event in the villages of the White Peak. Elaborate tapestries of flower petals are created and displayed around the village well. Look out for the individual village dates of the well dressings (for details, see www.visitpeakdistrict.com/whats-on/well-dressings).

There are some beautiful, quiet villages in the area, and these often have wonderful pubs and cafés that offer a welcome resting place. Parwich and Tissington are two excellent examples.

Lead mining played a major part in the life of the area from Roman times and became a major industry in the 19th century. The small town of Wirksworth became the centre of the lead-mining community and holds a wealth of history about the people who worked in the mines. The largest centre is Matlock which, along with Matlock Bath, runs along the Derwent Valley. The walk along Giddy Edge high above Matlock is a unique experience and one not to be missed if you have a strong head for heights.

WALK 21

Youlgreave to Elton

Start/Finish	Youlgreave YHA SK 209 642
Distance	6 miles (10km)
Ascent/Descent	230m
Time	3hr
Terrain	Minor country roads, open fields
Map	OS 1:25000 Explorer OL24
Refreshments	Youlgreave, Elton
Parking	Youlgreave, on-street parking

The walk starts in the busy village of Youlgreave (or Youlgrave), that bustles with shops, pubs and a range of accommodation. The walk takes you across typical limestone farmland and, in spring and summer, the meadows and hedgerows are carpeted with the colour and fragrance of wildflowers. The crystal-clear water of the River Bradford is full of wild trout; damselflies and dragonflies hover over every plant, while dippers hop-skip from stone to stone.

The Conduit Head water storage for Youlgreave

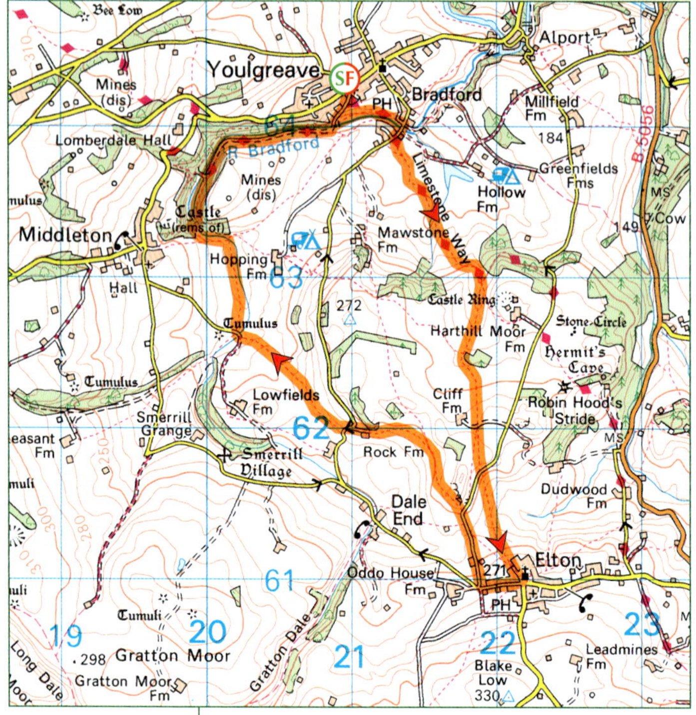

It is worth exploring **Youlgreave** before setting off on the walk. The circular stone structure opposite the YHA in Market Place is Conduit Head, a water tank that fed the village with drinking water from the springs at Mawstone. Behind it sits Thimble Hall, said to be the smallest detached house in Britain, with a width of less than 3.65 metres.

Starting from the YHA in **Youlgreave**, walk SW along Main Street and take the first road left and continue down past the village hall to the clapper bridge over the **River Bradford**. Do not cross the bridge but turn left through the gate and follow the **Limestone Way** downstream, eventually emerging through a gate onto tarmac. On your way down the track you will come across calm water just before a weir. ▸

Turn immediately right and cross the footbridge, go through a squeeze stile and along the path to a minor road. Go through a second squeeze stile then diagonally right up the road and cross to take the footpath, via a gate, running generally SE across fields, passing through four gates or stiles. Cross Bleakley Dike and ascend steps on the opposite side, then go through a gate into a field. Walk up the field maintaining a SE bearing, passing redundant stiles with no boundaries along the way. After the last wooden stile, go left to contour around the hillside along a farm track that eventually turns S alongside a hedgerow.

Continue past the access lane to **Harthill Moor Farm**, cross over three stiles and proceed uphill to the right of woodland, following the public footpath to Elton. The route follows the boundary of the wood SE until you meet a signpost pointing S. Follow the sign's direction across fields and through two stiles, then across the access lane to **Cliff Farm**, over a stone stile, then SE across fields and two stiles to come out through a hedgerow onto a minor road. Go directly across the road and through a gate into the meadow.

The **meadows** in this part of the White Peak are glorious in spring and early summer. The green carpet is festooned with campion, cowslips, harebells, meadow saxifrage and stitchwort. Butterflies flit from flower to flower – brimstones, orange tip, common blue and the red admiral are particularly abundant.

Follow the footpath down, heading S through two wooden gates before starting the ascent via two squeeze stiles to a farmhouse. Turn left then right by the farmhouse, out of the gate and follow the lane S past the church to arrive in **Elton** at the junction of Well Street and Main Street.

This wild swimming pool is especially enticing on a warm summer day.

Turn right along Main Street until you come to a public footpath on the right. Follow this down to the road then turn right along the road until it bends sharp right, heading NE at the village water troughs, known as Burycliffe Troughs. Go straight ahead through the squeeze stile into the woodland and follow the footpath past the old quarries then over a stone stile into open land. Go right heading for the rocky promontory on the skyline to meet a track by a large stone gatepost with a square hole. Walk NE across a field towards woodland following the signposts for Rock Farm. Go over a wooden stile and follow the footpath to emerge from the woodland via a metal gate onto a farm track. Continue along the track through several gates to **Rock Farm**.

The River Bradford

Follow the farm access track W until you meet a tarmac road. Go down the road and take the first footpath right across scrubland that can sometimes be wet, following power lines NW until the path veers left and exits farmland by the entrance to **Lowfields Farm**. Go right, over the bridge, and then right again across a stone stile, taking the footpath across fields following the course of a stream N past a derelict barn to arrive at the clapper bridge over the **River Bradford**.

Cross the bridge, noting the inscription on the stones, and go left along a footpath to metal steps. ▶

Descend the steps and turn right, following the footpath across a wooden footbridge to enter a limestone dale. Where the path forks, take the right-hand fork by the old sheep bridge, noting the 'books' chiselled into the stone wall.

The **Sites of Meaning** millennium project placed stone carvings around 17 points of access to the ancient parish of Middleton and Smerrill. Local people gathered quotations and words of interest to the locality and artists then turned these into inscriptions in stone at the access sites.

Bear left down the dale until you arrive back at the clapper bridge met at the start of the walk. Cross the bridge and go up the road then, at the junction, turn right into **Youlgreave** and to the YHA.

The stone clapper bridge with inscription is part of the Sites of Meaning project. This inscription is from Alexander Pope.

WALK 22

Middleton to Elton

Start/Finish	Middleton SK 195 631
Distance	9 miles (14.5km)
Ascent/Descent	385m
Time	4.5hr
Terrain	Minor country roads, footpath
Map	OS 1:25000 Explorer OL24
Refreshments	Elton
Parking	Middleton, on-street parking

Middleton by Youlgreave is one of those idyllic chocolate-box villages seldom visited but always admired. The honey-coloured stone houses around the village square are bedecked with flowers in summer. This walk visits some significant archaeological sites and rock features. The stone circle at Harthill has a wonderful outlook across fields. The hermit's cave nearby is also well worth a visit, as are the rocks of Robin Hood's Stride.

Note the inscription on the clapper stones. This is part of the Sites of Meaning millennium project that indicates the 17 ways into the village of Middleton by Youlgreave.

From **Middleton** village green, opposite the public toilets, go SE down the lane until it forks. Take the right-hand lane and follow the footpath over a wooden footbridge and up metal steps. Go right along the top of woodland until you come to a clapper bridge across the **River Bradford**. ◄

Go over the bridge and head SE, crossing the river again then rising E through fields towards trees. Go through the gate and continue in the same direction, following the footpath through a second gate to **Hopping Farm and Campsite**. Go through a gate onto the limestone chipping drive and then through the squeeze stile onto the campsite. Follow the fingerpost sign for Robin Hood's Stride across the campsite, exiting through a squeeze stile left along a fenced footpath. At the end of the path go through the stile and turn right up the steep

hill. At the top go through the gate and cross the narrow tarmac lane to another gate. Enter the field and initially follow the wall uphill then diagonally left as you near the top, then go over the stone stile. Keep SE on the footpath over six stiles and gates connecting several fields until you reach a wide farm track by the corner of enclosed woodland leading to Harthill Moor Farm.

Head left over two stiles and down the track then take the stile in the hedgerow on the right. Follow the footpath NE to a gate leading you through woodland. Exit onto a road then turn right uphill. Take the footpath left, opposite **Harthill Moor Farm**, and head for Robin Hood's Stride, crossing three stiles along the way. Note the stone circle in the field to your left.

Harthill Moor has a great deal to offer walkers interested in archaeology and the ephemera of the 20th century. **Nine Stone Close Circle** probably dates from the Bronze Age. The 2 metre-high stones, one with cup marks, are perfectly set against the White Peak landscape. Other stones lie close by but are not classified as part of the ancient monument. ◄

To the left of the track by Robin Hood's Stride a path leads through woodland to Cratcliffe Crag and the **Hermit's Cave**. This is very unusual and well worth a visit. ◄ To the right of the track, the gritstone outcrop of **Robin Hood's Stride**, a popular bouldering site, is full of intricately carved rock graffiti that is well worth exploring.

Continue through the gate to the left of Robin Hood's Stride down the track noting Hilary's Seat on the left. At the road, go straight across and follow the **Limestone Way** S up the ancient Portway passing **Dudwood Farm**. Take the next footpath right across the stile and through the hedgerow and continue SW across fields to a sports pavilion. Exit the field by a stile and walk up the lane to the right of the pavilion to enter **Elton**.

Turn right along Main Street through the village then go right by the church down Well Street. Take the left-hand fork just after the church through a farm gate and follow the signpost across fields to exit via a gate onto the road. Turn right then take the next footpath left, W over fields and rough ground. Cross five stiles or gates emerging via a final stile onto the road at **Dale End**. Go left and take the footpath right, by the telephone box, into **Gratton Dale**.

Walk along the dale until you come to a wall below a steep bank facing you. Go through the gate and then right, through the next one, to enter **Long Dale**.

To access the site, you need to seek permission from the nearby Harthill Moor Farm.

The cave is close to the ancient Portway so would have provided spiritual sustenance for travellers.

LIME PRODUCTION

There is a small limekiln at the bottom of Gratton Dale. Lime production has been an important activity in the region for centuries. Hundreds of small limekilns used to exist in the White Peak. The process is simple and remains essentially unchanged today for the production of cement in the huge quarries. Limestone and coal were placed in the kiln in alternate layers and were burnt. The resulting

The limekiln at the bottom of Gratton Dale

quicklime was raked out at the bottom. The product was used for building mortar, as well as for dressing fields and as an astringent in the tanning industry. While walking around the area you may hear a buzzer sound, followed a few minutes later by a muffled whump. This is the limestone being blown from the quarry faces.

Gratton Dale and Long Dale are two dry limestone valleys. Both are sites of special scientific interest (SSSI) because of the flora that inhabits the slopes and screes. Plants more common in the south of the country thrive here because of the aspect of the dales and the protection it provides. Spring sandwort and alpine pennycress can be found around the scree in Long Dale, while in Gratton Dale you can find mossy saxifrage and brittle bladder fern.

Proceed up Long Dale, passing through a gate as it widens. Continue until you come to a circular stone enclosure with standing stones in the centre. This is a Site of Meaning.

The **Sites of Meaning** are a millennium project that placed marker stones at the 17 entrances to Middleton by Youlgreave. Each marker has an inscription inspired by a local inhabitant. The stonework here is by Celia Kilner while the inscription is taken from a Nepalese teahouse menu! It reads, 'We meet to create memories and depart to cherish them'.

Bear right from here and follow the grassy track up the right-hand slope, then go through the gate at the top. Follow the wall line then track NE passing through two farm gates until a signpost directs you diagonally left, down a walled lane that eventually deposits you onto a road. Go left and follow this country lane back into **Middleton by Youlgreave**.

WALK 23

Middleton to Kenslow Knoll

Start/Finish	Middleton SK 195 631
Distance	4 miles (6.5km)
Ascent/Descent	190m
Time	2hr
Terrain	Minor country roads, open fields, bridleways
Map	OS 1:25000 Explorer OL24
Refreshments	Youlgreave
Parking	Middleton, on-street parking

This short walk is ideal for a mid-week or Sunday afternoon amble. With time on your side it is the perfect opportunity to visit some nearby landmarks. The resting place of Thomas Bateman, a Victorian barrow digger, is in the village of Middleton behind the converted Methodist church. Arbor Low, the Peak District Stonehenge, is also close by; it sits on private land but can be accessed for a small donation.

From **Middleton** village green, opposite the public toilets, go SE down the lane passing the farm on your right and, where the lane sweeps left, take the footpath right, through the gate in the hedgerow into a field. Turn left and follow the power lines E, through a gate, and on down to Rowlow Brook. Then turn right and head directly S across four stiles or gates, passing a derelict barn on the left. Continue S to cross a minor country road via a stone stile and enter the field opposite through a gate. Initially follow Rowlow Brook SW, passing a wonderful limestone outcrop on your right. Just after this, enter a field via a stone stile and turn right up the hill, keeping the wood on your right and passing through a squeeze stile with further outcrops nearby. Descend to a road.

Cross the road using the wooden stiles and walk up the field to a farm track. Where the land begins to level

Meadows filled with blossoming wildflowers are now returning to the White Peak and certainly brighten up any dull day.

out and the track sweeps right, go straight across the track to wooden steps near farm buildings. Go over the steps and across the paddock, then over the steps on the opposite side and through a metal farm gate. Ascend the steep hillside SW, keeping to the left of the hedgerow to reach a gate and stile. Cross another field then over a stone stile and turn right by **Mount Pleasant Farm**, going over the stone stile to the right of the farm gate. ◄

Continue straight on towards woodland, going through a wooden gate, and follow the track around until it meets with the farm access road. Go right up the access road, passing over a cattle grid to reach the road leading to Little Rookery Farm. Go straight on through a farm gate to the left of woodland and follow the wide track SW towards **Kenslow Farm**. At the next farm gate go left uphill following the signpost to **Kenslow Knoll**.

A topographic dial sits at the centre of the four avenues in this circular forest on **Kenslow Knoll**, known as the Millennium Wood. It indicates the location on the panoramic horizon of several important 'lows' (hills that are also ancient burial sites). Kenslow Knoll is sited on an ancient round barrow where artefacts from the Bronze Age and Roman periods have been found, included a dagger, a brooch and a battle axe.

Kenslow Knoll topographic dial

Retrace your steps to Little Rookery Farm and turn left down the walled lane towards **Middleton by Youlgreave**. Where the lane meets a road, turn right to return to the centre of the village.

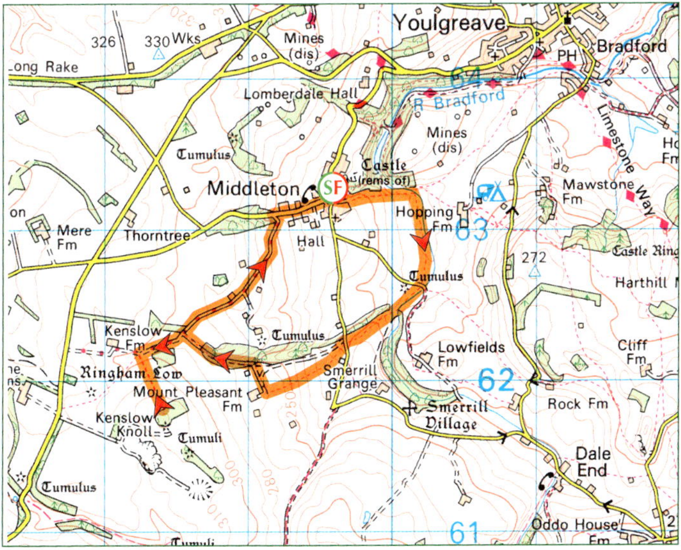

The tomb of Thomas Bateman, barrow digger and archaeologist

Thomas Bateman of Middleton Hall was an industrious, 19th-century barrow digger in and around the White Peak area. He excavated many sites and amassed a collection of ancient artefacts. Many of the finds are now in the museums of the cities surrounding the Peak District. His tomb, situated behind the converted Methodist church, is quite a sorry sight today and in need of much attention. Excavations by Thomas Bateman at Arbor Low revealed human remains and pottery.

ARBOR LOW

Arbor Low is the most important Neolithic henge monument in the area. It was in use between 2500 and 1500BC, with several developments of the site in that period. A large stone circle of more than 50 limestone slabs, once all vertical, sits within a circular bank and ditch. In the centre is the 'cove', thought to have been a stone box-like structure. Arbor Low's situation on high moorland enhances the sense of mystery and presence. The site sits on private land but can be accessed for a small donation. The monument is located 2 miles (3.5km) W of Middleton, near Parsley Hay national park visitor centre. Arbor Low grid reference is SK 162 636.

WALK 24

Winster to Bonsall

Start/Finish	Winster SK 241 605
Distance	8 miles (13km)
Ascent/Descent	480m
Time	4.5hr
Terrain	Minor country roads, footpaths
Map	OS 1:25000 Explorer OL24
Refreshments	Winster, Bonsall
Parking	Winster free car park SK 246 606

This walk takes you through the villages at the heart of this former lead-mining landscape. The industry is still much in evidence in the remains of the old workings and in the small villages that once flourished, thanks to the money lead brought into the economy. After visiting Winster and Bonsall, the route takes you into the beautiful Wensley Dale, one of the most peaceful dales in the Peak.

The small market town of Winster existed in some form before the Doomsday Book was compiled. The **Market House**, typical of its kind in these parts, has gone through various alterations, fluctuating with the fortunes of the town. Once the lead-mining industry ceased, the building fell into disrepair. It is now owned by the National Trust and contains a wealth of information on lead mining and the impact it had on the communities.

From the Market House in **Winster** walk S along East Bank and, where the road splits, take the left-hand fork following the road round until the houses on the left finish. Take the footpath to the right-hand side of the last house and ascend the short slope through a squeeze stile, continuing up to a gate leading into a lane along the Limestone Way.

Go through the gate and turn left down the **Limestone Way** to reach a gate across your path. Go through and walk a few metres, then take the footpath left, between stone gateposts, down the field to a signpost. Follow the signs for the Limestone Way in a SE direction uphill through nine gates or stiles to reach the minor road leading to Brightgate. Turn left and walk down the road to the footpath on the right, signposted for Bonsall. Go through the gate and walk up the field in a SE direction continuing across **Bonsall Moor** until you reach a gate leading into a lane. Go left a few metres then right at the lane junction and take the footpath signposted on the left through a gate. Cross several fields using squeeze stiles to narrow, walled enclosures with derelict barns. Cross both enclosures and then two further fields, exiting via a squeeze stile into a lane. Turn left along the lane and take the footpath on the right through a gate. Follow the line of a wall until you reach a gate on the left almost hidden at the junction of wall and fence.

Go directly E across fields to join the Limestone Way again via an ancient squeeze stile. Follow the Limestone Way across multiple fields, passing a barn on your right until you reach a gate facing across fields to farm buildings on the right. Cross the fields via squeeze stiles and enter Abel Lane in **Upper Town**. Turn right then left and follow the road down to a junction by a well on the left. Go left at the junction then immediately right, following the footpath between houses on Bell Lane, to enter a walled lane via a squeeze stile. Follow the footpath along the walled lane, passing through several squeeze stiles to descend into the centre of **Bonsall**. ▶

The World Hen Racing Championships are held in Bonsall each summer.

The Bonsall Cross with the Kings Head pub and former Queens Head pub behind

A good example of a market cross stands on 10 steps (or 13, depending which side you view it from) in the centre of **Bonsall**. Also on the square, the 17th-century Kings Head pub has wonderful mullioned windows. By the noticeboard you will find a replica of the lead miner T'owd Man; the original is on show in St Mary's Church, Wirksworth. A restored example of a weaving shed sits proudly on the hill, above.

Walk straight past the Bonsall Cross and over the road to take the lane past the information board into woodland. Follow the Limestone Way up a steep path as it winds its way up the hillside. Pass through a five-bar farm gate then, at the next farm gate, take the stile hidden in the hedge on the left into a field. Walk across two fields aiming for the wooden power pole in the distance, leaving the fields by a stile into a road. Cross the road and go over the stile opposite and head across the field to enter **Jughole Wood** via a gate. Follow the woodland path to a small quarry. Do not go over the stile into a field, but take the narrow footpath to the right of the stile that leads you above the quarry edge.

The cave is well worth exploring to see how the limestone formed the White Peak.

The footpath leads to a large cave. ◀ Continue following the footpath down through woodland, passing a fenced mineshaft on your right and exit into fields via a wooden gate. Walk down the field to gain the farm track. Go over the stile by the cattle grid, then bear right down the track and through the gate by a second cattle grid. Continue down the tarmac drive to the road at **Snitterton**.

Go right, then, at the split in the road, take the left-hand fork. At the next junction leave the road and take the footpath on the left across fields using several gates to enter **Wensley Dale**. Walk up the dale and take the second footpath right, uphill through a private garden and down a walled path leading into the village square of **Wensley**.

Go W across the square to the main road through the village and turn left, uphill. Just after passing the former Red Lion Inn, take the footpath on the right, up through

farmland aiming for trees on the left. Go past the trees and pond and exit via a gate onto a farm track by a holiday cottage that was formerly a water tank!

Take the gate opposite and follow the fence line right, around the field to a wooden stile leading into woodland. Follow the footpath NW down through the wood passing a pond on your right, eventually crossing a wooden footbridge over a small stream in the valley bottom. Follow the footpath to the track and turn left. Where the track swings left to a farm gate, go straight ahead into **Clough Wood** and follow the footpath beside the stream to a second footbridge. Cross the bridge and go through the gate, then follow the footpath up through the field to a wooden stile. Go over the stile and continue along the footpath, via squeeze stile and gate, to emerge through a final gate onto the road leading to **Winster**. Turn right and follow the road into the village and the Market House. ▶

The wonderful Wensley Dale

An interesting feature of Winster is the mixture of limestone and gritstone as a building material. The town sits on a geological boundary between the two types of rock.

WALK 25

Matlock to Dethick

Start/Finish	Matlock SK 297 595
Distance	7 miles (11.5km)
Ascent/Descent	470m
Time	4hr
Terrain	Minor country roads, footpath, edge traverse withexposure
Map	OS 1:25000 Explorer OL24
Refreshments	Matlock
Parking	Matlock car park SK297 595
Note	Giddy Edge is an exposed edge traverse. Do not attempt if you are afraid of heights or at all unsure

Matlock, the county town of Derbyshire, is not to be confused with Matlock Bath, a later spa construction and a place more akin to a resort. This walk features towering limestone cliffs and a frisson of excitement for more adventurous walkers who have a head for heights. The route takes you high above Matlock and across fields, passing through some wonderful villages to the remains of a strange mansion that once housed lynx cats.

From the car park in **Matlock** go N along the **A6** for 200 metres, then take the footpath right, over the **River Derwent** and railway line, to enter woodland. Follow the path E uphill until you reach a sign pointing the way to **High Tor**. Go right through the ornate gateway and follow the trail to the limestone precipice for magnificent views down into the valley below. As you arrive just below the summit, turn right by the information board and ascend steps to look out over Matlock and across to the Heights of Abraham. From this point the route splits: go left to the communications tower and the tarmac trail down through woodland; go right to walk along Giddy Edge, a narrow ledge that winds its way across the face of **High Tor**.

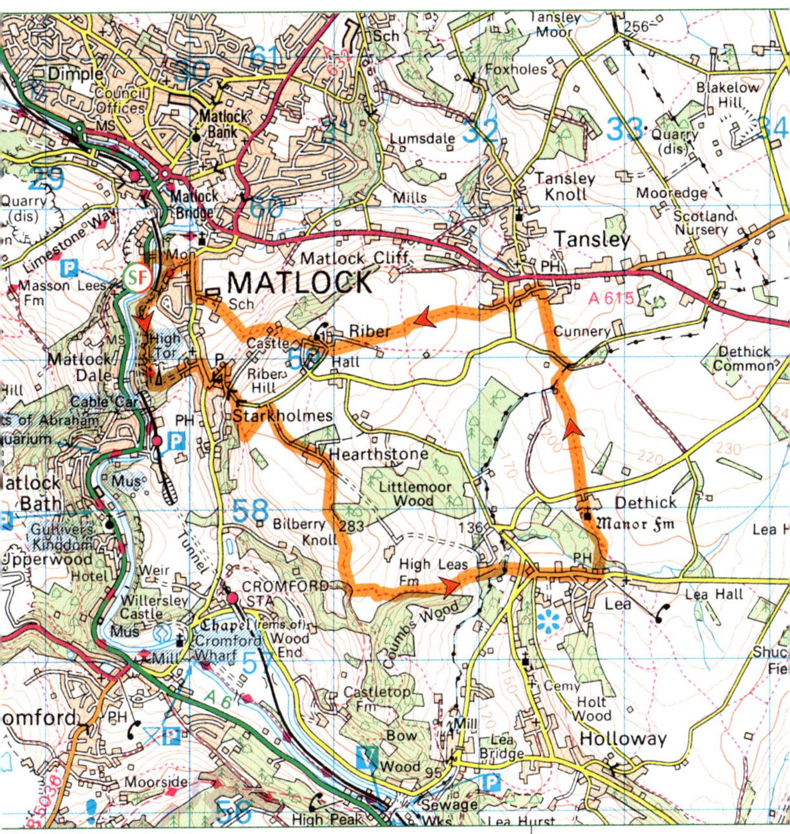

Please read the warning before attempting the traverse of Giddy Edge. There is no protection on the right from a fall. The route uses a one-way system; DO NOT ignore this. On the more exposed sections an iron railing is attached to the cliff face for added safety. From this high vantage point, the views across the Derwent Valley and directly down on the A6 trunk road are quite outstanding.

The narrow path along Giddy Edge

On reaching the end of the traverse, follow the steps down right to the picnic tables, then walk NE past the fenced chasm and follow the trail through a gate onto a residential lane. Walk to the road junction and turn right along the road until it splits. Take the left fork up Riber Road until you reach a signposted footpath on the right. Take this path S, with views of the ski lift on the opposite side of the valley, until you come to a wooden stile on the left. Go over the stile and across fields and two stiles heading towards Riber Castle and a minor road. Turn right down the road, through **Hearthstone** and, where the road becomes a trail, take the right-hand fork and follow Hearthstone Lane for 850 metres, then take the left-hand footpath over a wooden stile into fields. Follow the footpath over a second stile, along hedgerows skirting the

N edge of **Coumbs Wood**, and eventually descend to a wooden stile leading into woodland. Keep on the path as it winds its way down through the trees and crosses stepping-stones over Lea Brook. Cross the stile and ascend the lane to exit onto the road via a squeeze stile. Go right a few metres along the road then immediately left over a stone stile and up through the field to a stable. Go to the right of the stable through a squeeze stile and out onto the road then turn left into **Lea**. ▶

After the next road junction take the footpath left, signposted for Dethick, through a kissing gate, down to cross a bridge, then up steps and over a wooden stile into a field. Follow the wall on your left across the field heading for the church at **Dethick** on the horizon. Enter the churchyard and go right, then through a gate onto a minor road.

Anthony Babington of Dethick paid a heavy price for his Catholic loyalty. Enthralled by Mary, Queen of Scots he joined in a conspiracy to release her from Wingfield Manor, a few miles SE of the village. Sir Francis Walsingham, Queen Elizabeth's great protector, discovered the plot and Babington, along with his co-conspirators, were hanged, drawn and quartered at Lincoln's Inn Field, in London.

Florence Nightingale's family lived at Lea Hurst. The nearby village of Holloway was where she first became involved in caring for sick people.

The path to Dethick with the church on the horizon.

Go left to the junction and walk straight across. Follow the footpath up fields via four stiles or gates, maintaining the boundary wall on your left, to reach a narrow lane. Exit onto the lane via the stile and walk right to the road junction. Go left and take the footpath next right through the squeeze stile following the left-hand hedgerow. Go through a second squeeze stile in the corner of a wall and hedge and descend to go through another squeeze stile to a private driveway. Cross the tarmac to yet another squeeze stile opposite and follow the footpath down between houses to a minor road. Go left along the road and, at the next junction, go right, cross the road and take the footpath on your left, initially a tarmac lane then, via a squeeze stile, into a field to follow a drystone wall. Go right, through a second squeeze stile then W following a field boundary across fields and five gates or stiles to a walled lane. Go into the lane and turn right then immediately left through the squeeze stile in the opposing wall and follow the footpath across fields to the minor road at **Riber**. Turn right then left at the junction and walk up the lane to reach the gates of **Riber Castle**.

> **Riber Castle** has had an interesting if chequered history. It was built for John Smedley, the Matlock hosiery king, who enjoyed its splendour for a mere six years, before dying in 1874. The house and grounds then suffered various ignominies before becoming a sanctuary for wild lynx cats in 1962. This venture also foundered, and the castle stood empty again until this century, when it was purchased for luxury flats, only to be thwarted in its development yet again.

Take the footpath to the right of the gates, NW down the fields, exiting via a gate to reach a road in Old Matlock by a school. Go right and, just before the pub on your right, take the footpath opposite, initially up a walled tarmac lane. Then, at the entrance to **High Tor** encountered at the beginning of the walk, go right and retrace your steps to the car park.

WALK 26
Biggin to Minninglow

Start/Finish	Biggin SK 154 593
Distance	10 miles (16km)
Ascent/Descent	355m
Time	5hr
Terrain	Minor country roads, trails, footpaths
Map	OS 1:25000 Explorer OL24
Refreshments	Biggin
Parking	Biggin, on-street parking

Minninglow or (Minning Low), with its lofty setting, is perhaps the most imposing of the many ancient burial sites in the White Peak. The monument contains a Neolithic tomb and two barrows from the Bronze Age. The route from Biggin is a gentle amble along the High Peak Trail, with splendid views across the limestone landscape and a plethora of wildflowers and butterflies. The return journey along the dale from Roystone Grange is an unexpected delight.

From **Biggin**, walk E along Main Street to the **A515**. Cross the road and take the footpath, between wall and fence, to the left of the houses immediately in front of you. Go through a gate and cross the private garden, exiting via a second gate into a field. Follow the wall uphill, then go over a stone stile. Walk by the side of the left-hand wall to a fingerpost. Go over the stile continuing E heading diagonally left towards **Aleck Low** on the skyline. Go through a squeeze stile and head right over fields and three stone stiles to arrive at a wooden stile within a hedgerow. Cross the stile and the subsequent farm track and go left down the field to a stone stile leading onto the High Peak Trail above **Upperhouse Farm**. Go right and follow the trail over the **Pennine Bridleway**. Ignore the lane going down to Gotham but carry on, eventually passing through the **Minninglow car park** and across a minor road. ▶

As Minninglow Hill comes into view on the skyline, keep looking back along the curves of the trail to see the huge limestone embankments that were constructed to carry the rail line.

145

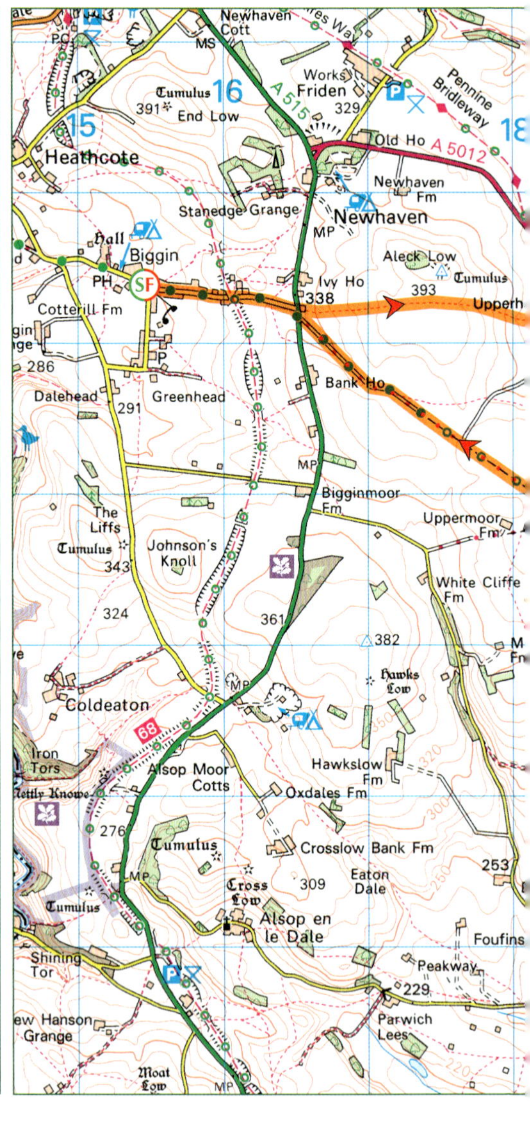

Newhaven Cott
MS
Cumulus 16
391 End Low
Works
Friden 329
Pennine Bridleway
15
Old Ho A 5012
18
Heathcote
Stanedge Grange
Newhaven Fm
Newhaven
MP
Hall
Biggin
SF
PH
Aleck Low
Cumulus
393
Ivy Ho
338
Upperh
Cotterill Fm
P
gin
ge
286
Bank Ho
Dalehead
291
Greenhead
MP
Bigginmoor Fm
Uppermoor Fm
The Liffs
Cumulus
343
Johnson's Knoll
White Cliffe Fm
324
361
382
ve
Hawks Low
Coldeaton
68
MP
Hawkslow Fm
Iron Tors
Alsop Moor Cotts
Oxdales Fm
ettly Knowe
276
Cumulus
Crosslow Bank Fm
253
Eaton Dale
Cross Low
309
Cumulus
Alsop en le Dale
Foufins
Shining Tor
P
Peakway
229
ew Hanson Grange
Parwich Lees
Moat Low
MP

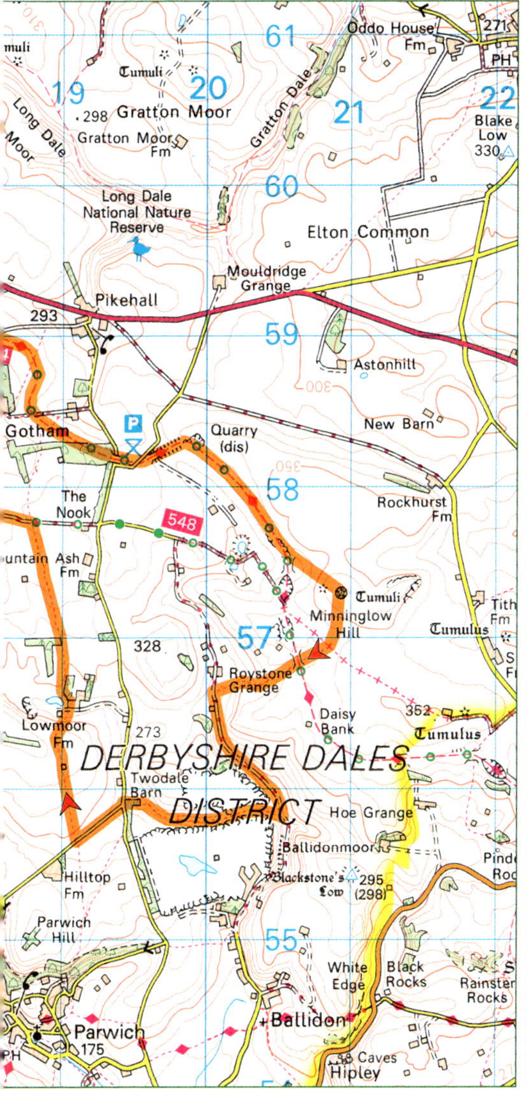
muli
19
Tumuli
20
.298 Gratton Moor
Gratton Moor
Fm
61
Oddo House
Fm
271
PH
22
Blake
Low
330
21
60
Gratton Dale
Long Dale
Moor
Elton Common
Long Dale
National Nature
Reserve
Mouldridge
Grange
Pikehall
293
59
Astonhill
300
Gotham
P
Quarry
(dis)
New Barn
350
58
Rockhurst
Fm
The
Nook
548
untain Ash
Fm
Tumuli
Minninglow
Hill
Tumulus
Tith
Fm
Tumulus
328
57
Roystone
Grange
Daisy
Bank
352
Tumulus
Lowmoor
Fm
273
DERBYSHIRE DALES
Twodale
Barn
DISTRICT
Hoe Grange
Ballidonmoor
Pind
Roo
Hilltop
Fm
Blackstone's
Low
295
(298)
Parwich
Hill
55
White
Edge
Black
Rocks
Rainster
Rocks
Parwich
175
PH
Ballidon
Caves
Hipley

Minninglow standing high above the surrounding landscape

Just after passing a small **quarry** on the left take the concession path towards **Minninglow Hill**. Go through the gate and follow the sign uphill to the summit and enter Minninglow by the NW gate. ◄

Minninglow contains the county's largest chambered burial tomb from the Neolithic period, as well as two Bronze Age bowl barrows. The site is raised and surrounded by a circular wall. Within the enclosure is a small copse as well as undisturbed remains. Thomas Bateman found human remains when he excavated the area in the mid 1800s.

Leave Minninglow by the SE gate and follow the signpost to take the footpath downhill and through a field gate to cross a lane. Go over the stone stile opposite and head for a gate that is above and to the right of the short underpass that supports the High Peak Trail. Pass through the gate and across the trail, and then go over the stone stile at the other side and continue across the field, keeping the wall to your right until you arrive at a squeeze stile. Squeeze through the wall and follow the left-hand boundary wall until you come to a stone stile. Go over the stile and follow the boundary wall, this time on your right, then go through a wooden gate. Turn left across the field to a stone stile leading onto a tarmac farm track to **Roystone Grange**.

Roystone Grange was originally built by the Cistercian monks of Leicestershire. Only the outline of the original medieval hall and barn now remains. The abbeys of England established many of the sheep farms in Derbyshire. The large building on the site is the former compressor house, that supplied air to drive rock drills in the local quarries when constructing the High Peak railway.

Follow the track down past the old compressor house to where the track sweeps left and splits. Take the right-hand fork uphill, crossing a bridge over a limestone quarry. ▶

Take note of the sign indicating that blasting will take place between 9am and 5pm; it's a common occurrence in the White Peak.

The sound of distant blasting in the quarries can often be heard. Never enter a quarry area when you hear the warning siren

Compressor house at Roystone Grange

Pass through a wall then, then just before the next wall that is straight ahead take the faint track left uphill towards trees. Go over a stone stile onto a minor road and turn left then immediately right at the junction. Walk along the road to a footpath on the right by a farm gate. Take this path, aiming to the right of woodland on the horizon and going over a stone stile on the way. Follow the right-hand wall until it descends towards **Lowmoor Farm**. Go over the stone stile on the right and walk diagonally left, downhill, to enter the farmyard via a gate. Turn left and follow the outline of the barn around two corners then take the footpath by the pond into a lane.

Turn left along the lane and then head through fields and five farm gates to a small wooded copse. Keep to the right of the copse and go over four stiles, following the footpath signs to finally enter a walled trail. Turn left along the trail heading NW. Take the right-hand trail at the fork through the gate until you reach the **A515**, passing Bank House on the left along the way. Retrace your steps into **Biggin**.

WALK 27

Cromford to Black Rock

Start/Finish	Cromford SK 300 570
Distance	5 miles (8km)
Ascent/Descent	265m
Time	3hr
Terrain	Minor country roads, footpaths, trail
Map	OS 1:25000 Explorer OL24
Refreshments	Cromford
Parking	Cromford SK 300 570

This is a wonderful heritage walk, taking in several important industrial sites. Cromford Mill, a World Heritage Site built by Sir Richard Arkwright, was one of the first successful industrial factory complexes in the world. The High Peak Trail was a former rail line that ran from Cromford Canal across the limestone country of the White Peak, using steam engines to pull trains up steep gradients. Climbing over 300 metres in 5 miles (8km), the line was a feat of engineering.

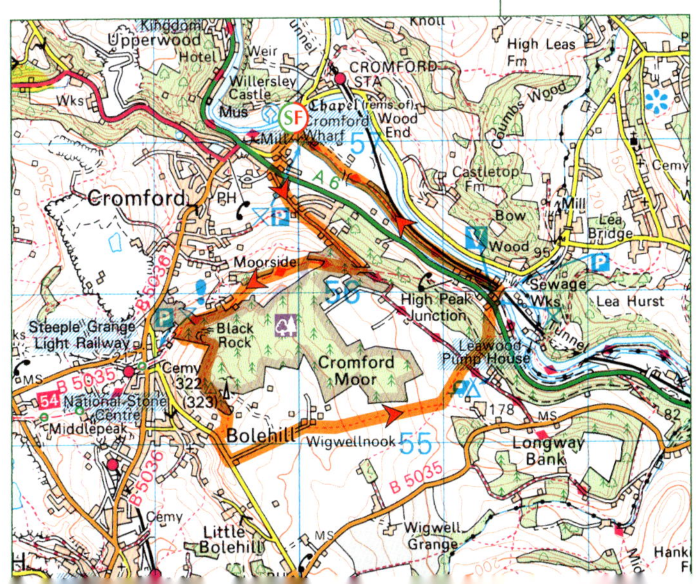

CROMFORD MILL

The rather austere Cromford Mill UNESCO World Heritage Site

Cromford Mill was a water-powered cotton-spinning mill built by Sir Richard Arkwright in 1771. It employed local workers in 12-hour shifts and, as was common in that period, many children helped maintain production. The 'water frame' that Arkwright invented produced a cotton thread strong enough to be woven. It was powered by water that drained from the surrounding lead mines via the Cromford Sough. Today the mill buildings and yard are little changed and can appear austere and somewhat derelict. However, in the summer months the area comes alive with visitor attractions.

Black Rock is a favourite with climbers who can be seen on almost any day performing gravity-defying feats.

From **Cromford Wharf**, turn left up the road and visit the **Cromford Mill** complex.

Return to the road and turn right. As the road sweeps right, cross over and take the footpath to the **A6** then cross into Intake Lane. Follow the lane uphill until it joins a track running up through woodland. Walk along the track until you pass underneath a **bridge**, then take a sharp right and follow the footpath up to the **High Peak Trail**.

Go left along the trail until you reach the car park for **Black Rock**. Turn left and walk along the footpath to the rock outcrop. ◀

Walk S to the walled boundary and turn left up the hill until you reach a short signpost. Turn right here and take the footpath up through the quarry to a gate leading onto moorland. Go through the gate and walk right towards the mast and **OS triangulation pillar**.

Continue SE past the OS pillar then through a gate to descend fields via a stile, eventually walking down stone steps and through a gate onto a road. Turn left up the road and then take the next lane left at the side of a low farm building. Follow the lane past **Wigwellnook** and through a gate, then veer right at a fingerpost just before the lane splits. Follow the path right, around the hawthorn hedge to a stile in a wall. Cross the stile and walk down through the fields keeping the wall line on your right, until you meet a gate across a walled lane. Take the small gate on the far left and follow the path across fields and four stiles to drop down onto Intake Lane.

Cross the lane and stile then go over a farm track, eventually entering woodland by a stile. Descend the holloway through the woodland into an open field via a gate. ▶

Head for the bottom corner of the field and exit via a stile onto the road. Cross the road and walk left then, just after a low barn, take the footpath right, down to **High Peak Junction**. Cross the canal and turn left to walk back to **Cromford Wharf**.

Created over hundreds of years, holloways – ancient ways up onto the moors or through the woodlands – are formed by the passage of thousands of feet and hoofs.

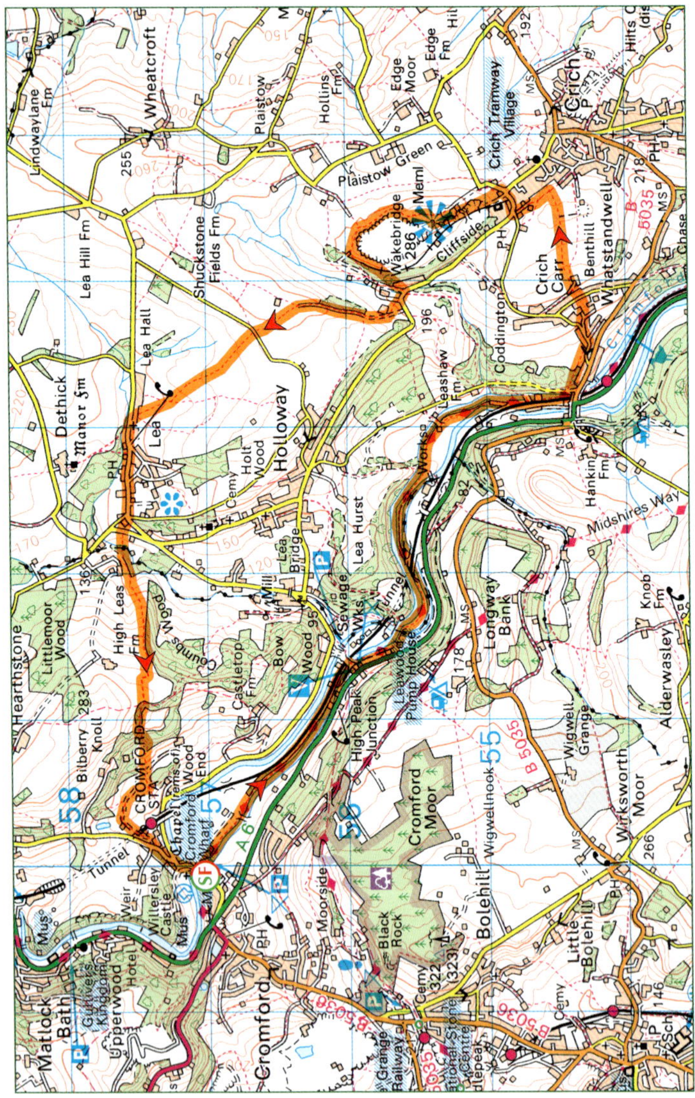

Wheatcroft
Lindwaylane Fm
Lea Hill Fm
Lea Hall
Dethick
Manor Fm
Hearthstone
Littlemoor Wood
Bilberry Knoll
283
High Leas Fm
Coombs Wood
Castletop Fm
CROMFORD STA
Cromford Wharf
Chapel (rems of)
Cromford Wood End
Tunnel
Weir
Willersley Castle
Mus
Matlock Bath
Gulliver's Kingdom
Upperwood
Cromford
Moorside
Black Rock
Cromford Moor
Wigwelnook
B 5035
Bolehill
Little Bolehill
266
Grange Railway
National Stone Centre
Middlepeak
Cemy
322
B 5036
146
Holloway
Lea
Lea Bridge
Holt Wood
Cemy
Lea Hurst
Bow Wood
95
Sewage Wks
Works
Lea Bridge Works
Lea Wood Pump House
High Peak Junction
178
Longway Bank
Hankin Fm
Midshires Way
Knob Fm
Alderwasley
Wigwell Grange
Wirksworth Moor
200
Leashaw Fm
196
82
Coddington
Crich Carr
Whatstandwell
Benthill
Shuckstone Fields Fm
Plaistow Green
Plaistow
Hollins Fm
Edge Moor
Edge Fm
Wakebridge
286
Meml
Cliffside
PH
Crich Tramway Village
Crich
192
218
Hilts
B 5035
Cromford Canal
255
260
170
200
150
136
120
150
95
57
58
55
56
A 6
B 5035
SF
MS

WALK 28

Cromford to Crich

Start/Finish	Cromford SK 300 570
Distance	8.5 miles (14km)
Ascent/Descent	440m
Time	4.5hr
Terrain	Minor country roads, footpaths, trail
Map	OS 1:25000 Explorer OL24
Refreshments	Cromford
Parking	Cromford SK 300 570

The Sherwood Foresters Memorial at Crich looks out across the White Peak and the eastern coast of Britain. On a clear day it is said that Lincoln Cathedral can be seen. This walk is unusual in the Peak District as it follows a canal, the Cromford Canal, from its terminus at Cromford Wharf to Crich. It is a lovely summertime walk in the cool of the shading trees.

From **Cromford Wharf** follow the canal towpath SE until you reach the road junction for Crich along the way passing the **Leawood Pump House**. ▶

At the road junction of the **B5035** turn left over the bridge then take the second left, Hindersitch Lane. Follow the road up and take the right-hand fork, then go right at the next junction until you reach stone steps leading up a narrow lane. Ascend the steps to the top and go right then left, following the signpost between houses up a very long flight of stone steps to a walled lane. Cross the lane and go through the squeeze stile opposite to enter a field. Follow the footpath across fields with fine views of the Crich Memorial on your left. Just after going through a tall squeeze stile, go over a stone wall and turn left and walk to a gate that eventually leads you between houses to a road. Turn right and cross the road past the entrance to **Crich Tramway Village**, then go straight on at the road

The Leawood Pump delivers 4 tons of water each stroke into the canal from the River Derwent. The pump is fully functioning and has public 'steam days' throughout the year.

The Leawood Pump House

The Crich Memorial is dedicated to the soldiers of the Sherwood Foresters Regiment who died in both world wars. From the top you can see eight counties and Lincoln Cathedral.

junction and immediately left through a gate. Follow the path to the entrance of the monument grounds. Walk up to the monument for the fine views. ◄

Take the footpath to the right of the steps at the foot of the monument and follow this around the quarry edge then straight across the tramlines. Descend through woodland along a narrow lane, going through a gate and bearing right by a danger sign denoting mine shafts. Continue downhill until a gate deposits you into a caravan park at **Wakebridge**. Go left down the park track until you meet a road.

Turn right, crossing the road for safety and, on the bend, take the footpath on the opposite side through the squeeze stile, heading right to farm buildings. Pass the buildings and walk up the lane, keeping left where it forks. Shortly after, the lane becomes walled on either side; take the footpath left across fields to a minor road. Go through the gate and straight across the road then over the stile. Head NW across fields via six stiles or gates, eventually dropping down into a holloway. Go right, down the lane, then almost immediately left up the banking and take the footpath across fields and four stiles, until you reach a lane. Walk down the lane and then left along the road at **Lea**, crossing to the opposite side where convenient. After exiting Lea, at the left-hand bend in the road take the footpath on your right by a small stable then head down the fields, exiting via a squeeze stile to a minor road. Cross the road and go over the stile opposite and walk down a narrow, walled path to cross the stream via stile and stepping-stones. Walk up the opposing stream bank to a fence, go left by the stile and follow the woodland path to a lane. Go through the stile and cross the lane to the opposing stile then walk up fields, W, following the path as it curves to the right, away from the woods, eventually leading onto a wide lane via a stile. Take the woodland path opposite downhill to reach a wall. Cross the farm track on the other side walking straight ahead into woodland. Turn right along the fence line dropping down the hillside until you exit onto a road. Go right along the pavement and return to **Cromford Wharf**.

WALK 29

Middleton to Harboro Rocks

Start/Finish	Middleton Top SK 274 551
Distance	7 miles (12km)
Ascent/Descent	320m
Time	4.5hr
Terrain	Minor country roads, footpath, trail
Map	OS 1:25000 Explorer OL24
Refreshments	Middleton Top
Parking	Middleton Top SK 274 551

The High Peak Trail, now a major cycling and walking route, was the rail line that carried limestone and freight between the Cromford and Peak Forest canals. The Middleton Top winding engine, which still runs periodically throughout the year, assisted the trains on the steep incline from Cromford. On the return leg, children of all ages will enjoy exploring the caves and rock formations at Harboro Rocks.

From **Middleton Top** walk E along the **High Peak Trail**, passing the engine house on the right.

Passing through a gate, walk down the incline and on the left you will pass the **National Stone Centre**, which is well worth visiting if time allows. ◄ Keep on the trail, passing the light railway at **Steeple Grange**, then walk across two bridges spanning roads. Shortly after the second bridge, take the footpath on the left down to the road. Cross the road and turn right along the pavement until you reach a footpath on the left, just past the cemetery. Turn left here and take the footpath across open ground and a road then through a small industrial estate to reach a gate leading to Gang Mine Nature Reserve. Follow the footpath through the reserve, exiting opposite a farm track that would lead you to **Pearsons Farm**. Walk to the right of the track and take the footpath to the left of the

The centre has examples of drystone walling, carvings and the different types of stone that are available.

Middleton Top Engine House

Middleton Top was one of eight engine houses along the High Peak rail line. There was a difference in altitude of 300 metres between the Cromford and Peak Forest canals and the high moorland that the line stretched across. Long, steep inclines were built to haul freight up, powered by these engines. An endless steel rope, feeding from the engine house via a wheel pit (that can be viewed just past the gates), was attached to the wagons, raising or lowering the line freight along the incline. Today only Middleton Top, with its double beam steam engine, survives intact.

enclosed land across open ground to a narrow lane. Walk up the lane, passing the church on the left and, at the road junction, turn left into Chapel Lane in **Middleton**. At the next junction go straight ahead between houses opposite, following the lane uphill, keeping right all the way until it becomes a track. Follow the track uphill; note that its location differs to that of the OS map. As you reach the top, go right along another track carrying straight on, as it becomes a tarmac lane.

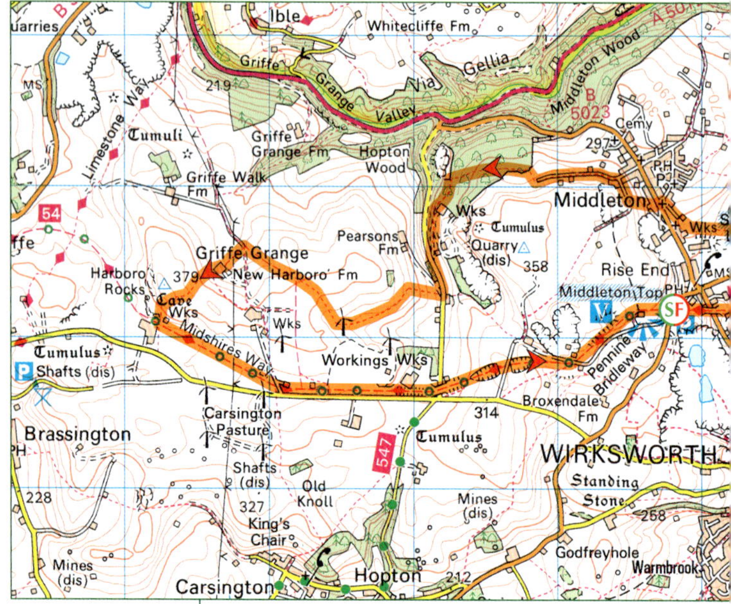

Do not attempt to approach or enter the mine. A system is in operation that will sound buzzers and bring forth security personnel.

Turn left at the junction with a road and follow it uphill until it becomes a track. Continue along the fenced track as it progresses by fields and then turns sharp right downhill. Go left at the bottom and follow the footpath through woodland until you reach the road to Hopton Mine. ◄

Walk ahead S to the road. Turn left up the road for 500 metres then cross and take the footpath over the stile W up the field. Go over the wooden stile at the top and cross the fields heading for two wind turbines. Near the first wind turbine, cross a stile and walk right, up a walled lane, emerging onto a farm track. Turn right and follow the track NW across three stiles towards **Griffe Grange** and **New Harboro Farm**. Turn left towards the farm along the footpath, turning right then left as you reach the gate to the farmhouse. Turn left uphill and cross two stone stiles to reach **Harboro Rocks**.

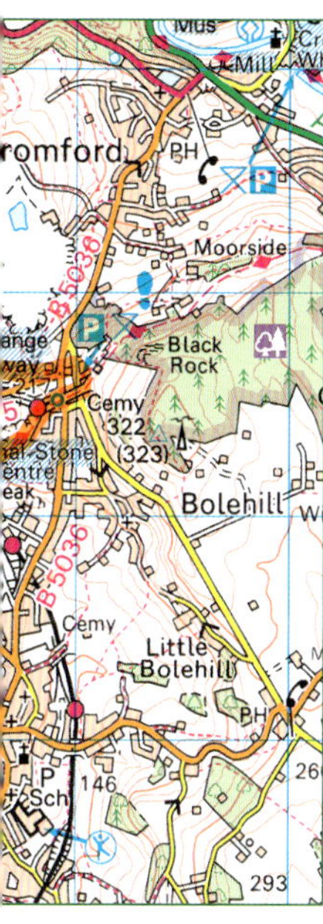

The **cave at Harboro Rocks** can be accessed from above or below. You can also see a massive rock chair. The views from the Ordnance Survey triangulation pillar across the White Peak are extensive. The rather space age-looking concrete structures below the rocks were part of lead ore workings that functioned here and are interesting to explore; but take care.

Descend SW from the left of Harboro Rocks onto open ground then through a squeeze stile onto the High Peak Trail. ▶ Turn left and walk along the trail crossing two roads and descending the Hopton Incline to return to **Middleton Top**.

The High Peak Trail runs for 17 miles (27km) from Cromford to Dowlow near Buxton. It is used by walkers, cyclists and horse riders.

Harboro Rocks

WALK 30

Brassington to Kniveton

Start/Finish	Brassington SK 233 546
Distance	11 miles (18km)
Ascent/Descent	450m
Time	6hr
Terrain	Minor country roads, footpath, trails
Map	OS 1:25000 Explorer OL24
Refreshments	Brassington, Carsington, Hognaston, Kinveton
Parking	Brassington car park SK 233 546

The countryside bordering the Peak District can be just as exceptional as the national park itself. This walk takes in some of the most beautiful villages in the Derbyshire Dales, with the added bonus of Carsington Water, a significant location for birdspotting. The route takes you across gently rolling countryside and through pretty villages with wonderful churches and pubs. It is a walk best enjoyed in dry, warm weather.

From the car park above **Brassington**, walk SW to the road junction, then go left down Dragon Hill into the village. Just before reaching Miners Hill on your right, take the footpath left between houses. Cross two fields using stiles then turn left and follow the wall line uphill, through the squeeze stile at the top. Turn right along the path initially S then SE, past old mine workings, to a farm track. Follow the track to a stile and cross the lane to the opposite stile and enter the next field. Walk E keeping parallel to the windmills on your left until you reach a wooden stile in the fence corner. Cross the stile and follow the clear grassy track SE, keeping right where it splits at a gate. Go through the gate to a tarmac lane. Enter **Carsington**, going straight on at the junction then keeping right where the road forks. Just after the pub take the road on your right, SW, to cross the busy **B5035** and enter the land surrounding **Carsington Water**. Go straight ahead and follow the red waymark arrows to the visitor centre, keeping the reservoir on your left. There are several bird hides along the path to the **visitor centre**. ▶

Continue SW until you find yourself walking beside a hawthorn hedge. Maintain the direction until you reach the signpost pointing right to the road. Follow the sign's direction across the road, go over the stile opposite, then walk W. Halfway up the field, go through a gate and veer SW across the field to reach two stone gateposts standing on their own in line with an ancient hedgerow. Pass the posts and go S along the hedgerow, then go W after passing through the next hedge. Exit through a squeeze stile into a narrow lane and head S to a road junction. Turn right, uphill, to a minor road. Go left and follow the road up a steep incline to arrive in **Hognaston**.

At the church junction go left, then right at the bus stop. Walk along the driveway, taking the public footpath to the right of the first house and following the fence line

Birds often found around Carsington include kingfishers, great crested grebes and tufted ducks.

HOGNASTON CHURCH

Hognaston church is well worth exploring. There has been a church on this site since Norman times. In the medieval period, villagers used the church as a refuge against marauders. They would secure themselves in the tower; you can still see the slits where they would endeavour to repel the attackers. Inside the church, Blue John

The tympanum above the doorway of Hognaston church

stone, from the mines around Castleton, has been used around the pulpit. Above the door the tympanum shows a bishop with animals including a lamb with a cross, a fish and the Hognaston hog.

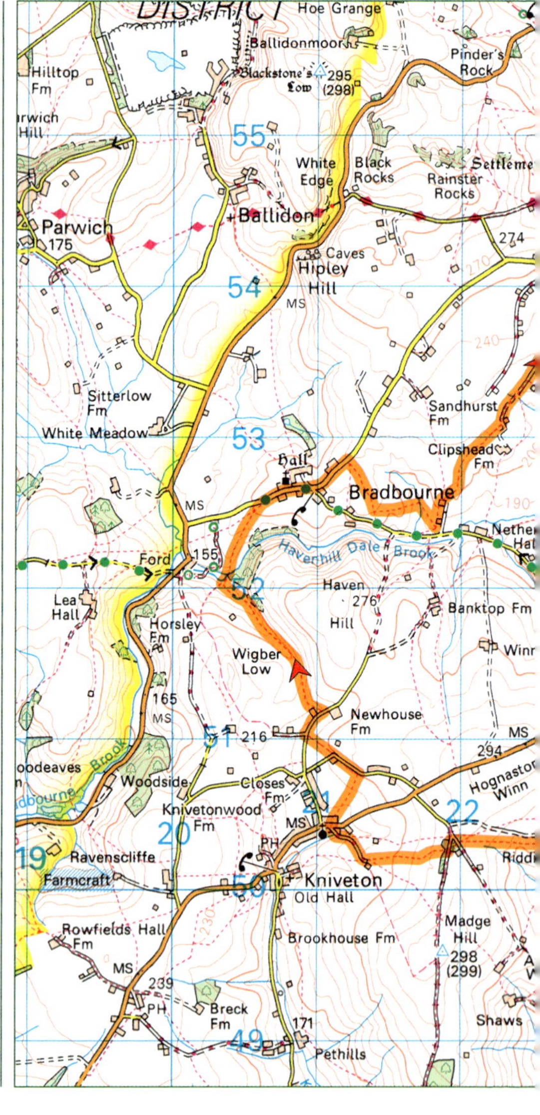
DISTRICT
Hoe Grange
Ballidonmoor
Pinder's Rock
Hilltop Fm
Blackstone's Low 295 (298)
arwich Hill
55
White Edge
Black Rocks
Settlement
Rainster Rocks
Parwich 175
Ballidon
274
270
Caves
Hipley Hill
54
MS
240
Sandhurst Fm
Sitterlow Fm
Clipshead Fm
White Meadow
53
190
Hall
Bradbourne
MS
Haverhill Dale Brook
Nether Hall
Ford 155
Haven
276
Banktop Fm
52
Lea Hall
Horsley Fm
Haven Hill
Wigber Low
Winn
165
MS
Newhouse Fm
MS
51 216
294
Brook
Hognaston Winn
oodeaves
Woodside
Closes Fm
22
19
adbourne
Knivetonwood Fm
21
MS
Ridd
20
PH
Ravenscliffe
Kniveton
Farmcraft
58
Old Hall
Madge Hill
Rowfields Hall Fm
230
Brookhouse Fm
298 (299)
MS
239
A V
PH
Breck Fm
171
Shaws
49
Pethills

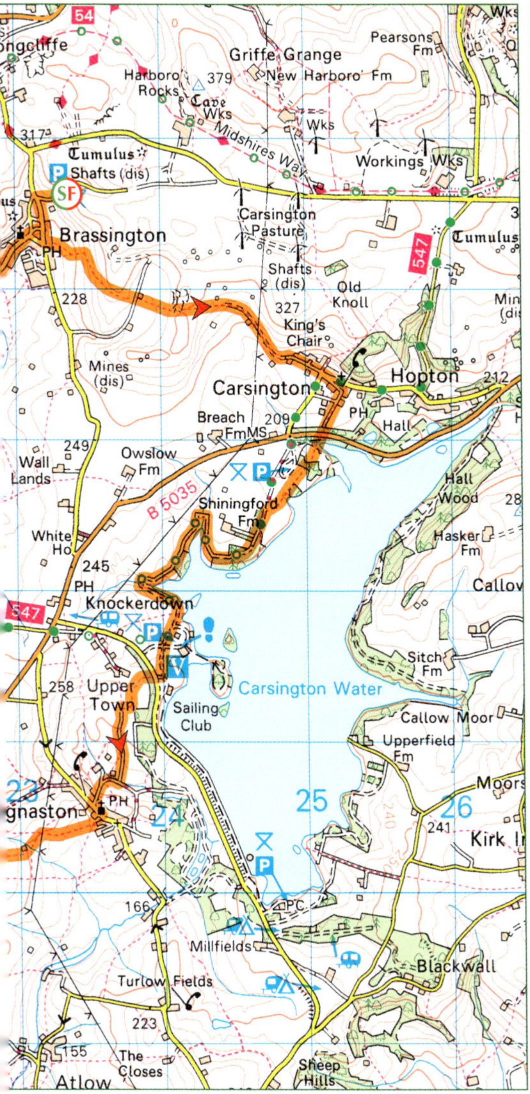

54
ngcliffe
Griffe Grange
379
New Harboro' Fm
Pearsons Fm
Wks
Harboro Rocks
Cave Wks
Midshires Way
Wks
Workings Wks
317
Tumulus
Shafts (dis)
SF
Carsington Pasture
547
Tumulus
3
Brassington
PH
228
Shafts (dis)
327
Old Knoll
Min (dis)
King's Chair
Mines (dis)
Hopton
212
Carsington
Breach Fm MS
209
PH
Hall
249
Owslow Fm
Hall Wood
28
Wall Lands
B 5035
Shiningford Fm
Hasker Fm
White Ho
245
Callov
PH
Knockerdown
Sitch Fm
547
Carsington Water
258
Upper Town
Sailing Club
Callow Moor
Upperfield Fm
23
Moors
24
25
240
26
241
Kirk I
gnaston
PH
166
PC
Millfields
Blackwall
Turlow Fields
223
155
The Closes
Atlow
Sheep Hills

W through a gate. At the corner of the hedgerow go right towards a pylon, then over a wooden stile, keeping to the right of the power lines, and cross a brook via a footbridge. Walk straight ahead up the short banking, then through a gate and up towards farm buildings. Follow the footpath to the right of **Riddings Farmhouse**, then go right at the top and left at the gateway, up the short lane. At the top of the lane go through the gate and head W across fields, through three gates to a minor road. Turn right then, soon after, go left, skirting a small copse. Just after clearing the wood, follow the footpath right through four field boundaries using stile or gate on an indistinct footpath to a lane. Follow the lane NW to cross the **B5035** at

Remains of the Saxon cross in Bradbourne church

Kniveton. Go through the gate to the right of the school and follow the path past the playing fields and through two gates to a narrow lane. Go left and, where the lane turns sharp left, carry straight on over a stile and, keeping NW, cross the field to a tarmac lane. Go right towards **Newhouse Farm** and take the next footpath left through a narrow gate, down into a wide dale. Follow the path along the dale bottom then cross over the stream via two footbridges and ascend NE through fields and squeeze stiles to reach the road into **Bradbourne**. ▶

> **Bradbourne** is one of only 15 Doubly Thankful villages in the country, and the only one in Derbyshire. Doubly Thankful villages lost no men or women in either the First or Second World War. All Saints' Church is well worth a visit and contains Derbyshire marble from Ashford in the Water.

Turn right and walk through the village. After the last farm on the left take the footpath SE across fields towards the remnants of an old hedgerow. About 100 metres before the hedge meets the road, walk due E through the remnants of a second hedgerow. Cross the field then a small brook and go SE towards a stone house. Before reaching the house follow the field boundary NE up the field and past a second house then go right, across further fields and gates, to the farm track leading to **Clipshead Farm**. Turn left down the track and follow this into **Brassington**. At the junction in the village turn right and follow the main road through the village. Where it splits, bear left and, at the next junction, go right and retrace your steps to the car park.

Bradbourne churchyard is the resting place of actor Alan Bates.

WALK 31

Parwich to Alsop en le Dale

Start/Finish	Parwich SK 189 542
Distance	5.5 miles (9km)
Ascent/Descent	225m
Time	3hr
Terrain	Minor country roads, open fields, trail
Map	OS 1:25000 Explorer OL24
Refreshments	Parwich
Parking	Parwich car park SK 189 542

Parwich was voted one of the best places to live in Britain in 2016 because of its beauty and isolation. It is an idyllic setting with the quaint pub acting as the backdrop to the village green and pond, all overseen by the large country house sitting in formal gardens. This route gently takes you over dales to the village of Alsop en le Dale, whose fine church contains superb stained-glass windows.

In 2008 the Sycamore Inn became one of the first pubs in Britain to include a village shop. Walkers are made welcome in both the shop and the pub.

From the car park turn left and walk up the main road, passing between the pub and the village pond, then take the public footpath left in front of cottages, then right between the buildings to emerge onto a road. ◄

Go left and follow the road until it sweeps right, then take the footpath through a gate and bear right up through two fields exiting through a gate and squeeze stile into a narrow lane. Go straight ahead over the next stile and walk across fields through seven stiles or gates, heading W then NW to a tree-lined lane to the SW of **Parwich Lees**. Cross the lane and follow the footpath up the dale until, shortly after crossing a farm track, you enter a field by woodland via a stone stile. Walk along the boundary fence of the wood on your right then go through the gate and follow the path down through the wood and out into a field. Go left and over the stone stile, then bear right and aim for the squeeze stile immediately below a house.

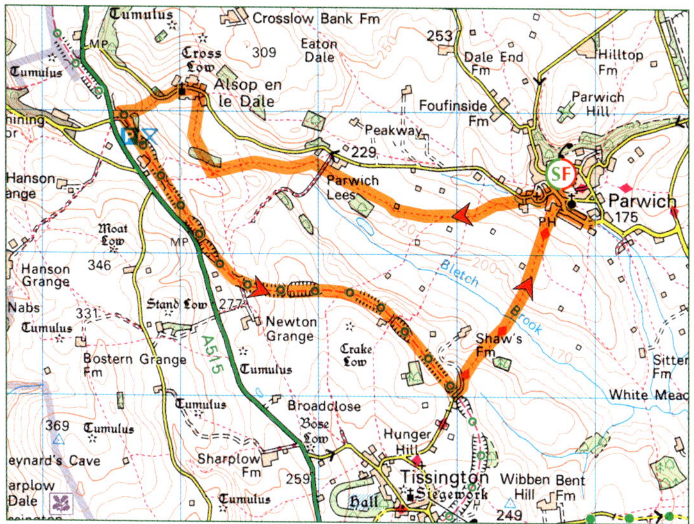

Walk up the public footpath to the left of the house, then turn left along the road to the church in **Alsop en le Dale**.

St Michael's Church dates back to the Norman period. The doorway is particularly fine, with its unusual zigzag voussoirs. The tower is not original but was added in the late 1800s. Inside there is a wonderful floor of Minton encaustic tiles and an intricately carved pulpit that once resided in the church at Ashbourne. The highlight, however, is the stunning stained-glass window by Henry Haig, installed for the millennium and based on Revelations 21 and 22.

Carry on along the road past the church and, as the road bends sharp right, take the footpath on the left up the field, following the wall on the right. Go through the squeeze stile in the wall and continue up the next field, now with the wall on your left, until you reach the **Tissington Trail**.

The Henry Haig Millennium Window in St Michael's Church, Alsop en le Dale

Go left and follow the trail for 2 miles (3.3km) until you reach the **Limestone Way** by a railway bridge that has an old rail signal attached to it. Go under the bridge and take the footpath right up to a lane then walk right across the bridge and follow the farm track to the public footpath signpost pointing to Parwich.

Follow the sign's direction, keeping to the Limestone Way down fields then through a squeeze stile and continue with the hedge on your left until you cross a wooden footbridge over **Bletch Brook**. At the other side of the footbridge walk uphill, then over a stile and wooden bridge to follow the footpath NE over fields to a corner where a squeeze stile hidden in the hedgerow gives access to open fields directly above **Parwich**. Walk due N down the field through a squeeze stile in a wall, then turn right along the wall to a wooden stile. Cross over the stile and enter a narrow lane that will lead you back to the village green. Turn left along the front of the cottages then right and walk back to the car park.

WALK 32
Parwich to Tissington

Start/Finish	Parwich SK 189 542
Distance	6.5 miles (10.5km)
Ascent/Descent	300m
Time	3.5hr
Terrain	Minor country roads, open fields, trail
Map	OS 1:25000 Explorer OL24
Refreshments	Parwich, Tissington
Parking	Parwich car park SK 189 542

The village of Tissington is mentioned in the Doomsday Book and has been in the same family since the mid 1400s. The present house was built in the 1600s and is a fine example of Jacobean architecture. Every year, the wells that supply the village are dressed on the eve of Ascension Day, a tradition that draws tens of thousands of visitors. The interior of the Norman church reflects the family ownership of the village over the centuries to the present day.

From the car park in **Parwich** turn left and walk up the main road, passing between the pub and the village pond, then follow the public footpath left in front of cottages, ignoring signs for the Limestone Way. Walk along the track and, just before entering a private driveway, turn right along the footpath. Go over the stile and bear left through a squeeze stile then up a field to a second squeeze stile hidden in the hedgerow. Squeeze through and follow the **Limestone Way**, with a hedge on your right, across fields to a wooden footbridge with a stile. Cross the bridge and drop down to the bottom of the dale, then across a second footbridge over **Bletch Brook** and ascend the hill to a farm track leading to **Shaw's Farm**. Go left up the track and cross a stone bridge, then take the footpath left down to the Tissington Trail. ▶ Go left for 700 metres then, just before a bridge, take the

The Tissington Trail is for use by walkers, cyclists and horse riders. To avoid confusion and collision always keep to the left and be nice and say hi.

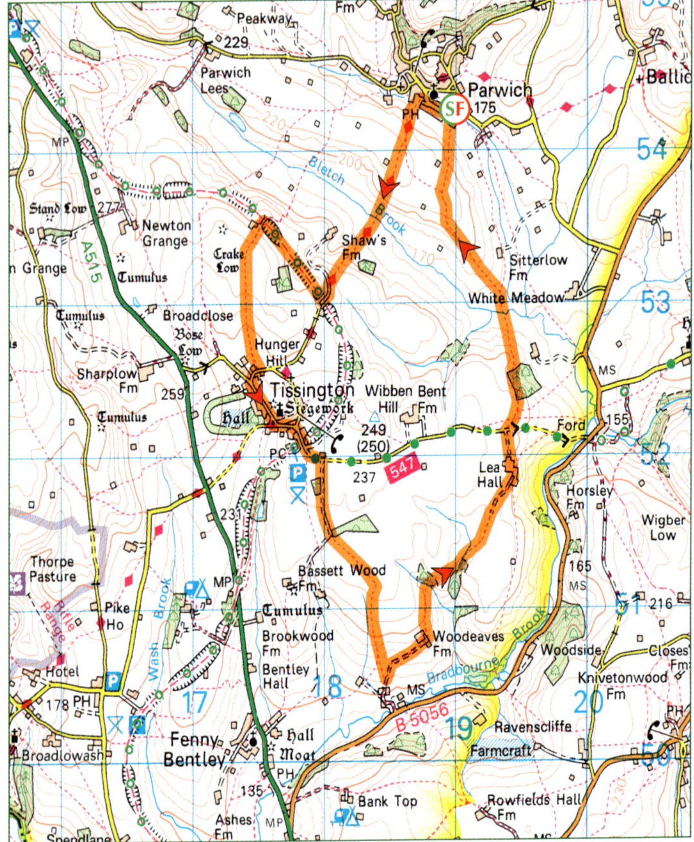

footpath on the right through the gate and walk across the bridge to continue over the trail along a track.

Where the track forks at the farm bear left then go through a farm gate. Cross a field to a stone stile over a wall, then continue across a succession of fields and two gates S until you reach Chapel Lane, by the Edwardian sweet shop. Go right, down the lane and left at the junction to enter **Tissington**.

The Edward and Vintage sweet shop in Tissington will take every child back in time

TISSINGTON

Tissington is a delightful village. The Fitzherbert family have owned the estate since the late Middle Ages. The house dates from the 1600s but the houses in the village are much later, mostly 19th century. Well dressing takes place each year, when the wells supplying water to the village are adorned with intricate panels of clay depicting religious and non-religious scenes picked out in flower petals. The panels stay in place for one week. The Norman church is worth exploring. You can trace the generations of the Fitzherbert family from the monuments and tombs inside the church.

Walk past **Tissington Hall** and go left at the next junction. Pass the village duck pond on the right and bear right where the road forks. Continue between the entrance to the Tissington Trail car park and a row of cottages on the left to exit the village across a bridge over the trail.

After crossing a cattle grid, walk along the road and take the farm road on the right towards **Basset Wood Farm**. Where the road sweeps right just after a cattle grid, take the farm track straight ahead. Eventually the track becomes a footpath across fields and three gates, heading first SE then S to a farm track leading to **Woodeaves Farm**. Go left and follow the fingerpost NE up the track through the farm, then take the footpath on the right through the gate as you exit the farmyard. Follow the path N over a stile and across fields to a gate leading to a wooden bridge over a stream in a narrow ravine. Cross the bridge then walk up the other side to a gate into a field. Go left over a stile and cross a field aiming for the fingerpost in the corner. Pass through the hedgerow to a gate then bear left along the hedge to a second gate. Follow the field sidetrack that takes you NE. Where the track splits take the right-hand fork across a cattle grid to **Lea Hall**.

Walk along the footpath between farm buildings following the signs for Parwich. After leaving the farm, go over the cattle grid and, where the tarmac track meets a minor road, bear NE across a field to a gate. Go N through the gate following the hedgerow through two gates and a stile until you drop down to cross the bridge at **Bletch Brook** near **White Meadow**. Cross the meadow, then go left and follow the footpath uphill across five stiles. At the top of the hill go N descending the other side to a squeeze stile. Cross a final field before entering a house drive that you exit via electronic gates to find yourself back at the car park in **Parwich**.

WALK 33

Wirksworth to Alport Height

Start/Finish	Market Place, Wirksworth SK 286 539
Distance	9 miles (14.5km)
Ascent/Descent	480m
Time	4.5hr
Terrain	Minor country roads, open fields
Map	OS 1:25000 Explorer OL24
Refreshments	Wirksworth, Alderwasley
Parking	Market Place, Wirksworth, SK 286 539

The small town of Wirksworth is full of winding streets and buildings seemingly tumbling down hillsides. It was formerly the administrative centre of the lead-mining industry. Disputes between mine owners were settled at the Barmote Court that still meets twice a year in the centre of town. Alport Height provides the highlight of the walk, with views across the midland planes of England to the Malvern Hills.

From Market Place in **Wirksworth**, walk N along St John's Street then turn right down Coldwell Street. Just opposite the first junction on the left, follow the narrow lane into the churchyard of St Mary's.

ST MARY'S CHURCH

St Mary's Church was extensively restored by George Gilbert Scott in the 19th century. The oldest surviving parts of the original church date back to 1272 when the first clergy was appointed. The Norman font and Anglo-Saxon coffin lid are well worth seeking out. The coffin lid, known as the Wirksworth Stone, dates from around the ninth century and has intricate carvings depicting the life of Christ. The church also contains the original T'owd Man, the lead miner relocated here from Bonsall. The ancient practice of 'clipping' takes place here on the first Sunday after the Feast of the

Nativity of the Blessed St Mary. This involves the congregation surrounding the church and holding hands facing outwards then dancing to hymns and religious songs. The word 'clipping' derives from the Anglo-Saxon work *clyppan*, meaning 'to embrace'.

Stone coffin complete with drain channel in Wirksworth churchyard

Retrace your steps and continue down Coldwell Street. After crossing the rail bridge turn left and walk up the short road until it meets a dead end at some houses. Go to the left of the houses and take the footpath N, following the rail track, then go over a stile and diagonally right to cross a second stile. Walk straight on and drop down to cross a footbridge over a stream, then walk up a narrow field to the top boundary. Go left, following the marker post through the hedge and then right up the field. At the top bear left by a wooden stile and follow the footpath diagonally up to a narrow road at **Little Bolehill**. ▶ Turn left along the road then, just prior to the telephone box at the next junction, go right following the fingerpost sign up the steep tarmac road. Where the footpath's handrail ends go left following the waymark up a narrow lane emerging via steps onto a road. The route

The name 'Bole Hill' implies a windy location, perfect for lead smelting as the wind forces oxygen into the smelter to melt the lead.

was used by workers from Wirksworth to the 'boles' at the top of the hill.

Turn right and walk along the road until you reach a low barn on the opposite side of the road. Cross here and follow the bridleway past **Wigwellnook Farm**, then go over a stile until it forks at a fingerpost. Follow the bridleway right down a holloway, then down fields until you reach a farm gate at the entrance to a narrow lane. Go through the small gate to the far left of the lane entrance, then walk diagonally across the narrow field, over the stone stile, and follow the wall line NE to reach a tarmac lane. Go right and walk along the lane until it meets the **B5035**.

Walk directly across the road and follow the **Midshires Way** up **Longway Bank** into the walled footpath that rises along the side of woodland. Follow the footpath through the wood and exit via a series of stiles to the left of farm buildings. Then follow the concrete farm track downhill until the unmade track sweeps left. Take the footpath on the right through stiles and gates then alongside a small stream until you arrive at the entrance to a farm. Cross the concrete track and go over a stile then diagonally left to walk through a small picket gate and go straight ahead uphill to a second gate that leads into a field. Follow the left-hand hedgerow and, at the top, take the Peak and Northern Footpath directions for **Alderwasley**, crossing stiles and gates until you reach a minor road.

Go right and walk up the hill past the junction and, as soon as the road becomes Higg Lane, take the footpath right, down through woodland and across the stone bridge to a farm track. Bear right along the track until it ends at a farm then go right over a wall and take the public footpath along the edge of woodland exiting onto a narrow lane. Go right and follow the lane until it ends facing a cottage. Go left through a squeeze stile and follow the left-hand boundary across fields to a minor road. Turn right down the road and, where it sweeps right, go left along the footpath into a field beyond a house on your left, following the signpost for Alport Height. Just before reaching the top of the third field go diagonally left to cross a stone stile into a field and, maintaining the same course, exit into the Bear Inn car park.

Exit the car park and cross the road to the gate leading into a field, and follow the path, keeping the boundary to your right, until you exit onto a lane. Go right and, at **Clearsprings Farm**, keep to the left of the buildings and go through a gate and across a field to the left of a house. Go across the house yard onto the drive and, just past the house, go through the gate into the field and along the footpath, heading SW by the left-hand hedge to emerge via a stile onto a minor road. Go left and then right at the entrance to Roughpiece Farm, over the stile and follow the boundary along the permissive path to a minor road. Go right along the road then left at the next junction to reach **Alport Height**. ▶

Take the footpath opposite the car park entrance down to the minor road, then follow the road downhill and, where it sweeps left, take the right-hand footpath down through fields exiting onto a road via the very narrow footpath at the right of a water treatment station. Follow the road down then, just after crossing a stream, take the footpath left up through a garden and out onto a field by

On a clear day the panorama from Alport Height is spectacular, stretching southwest to Shropshire, Herefordshire and Gloucestershire. The Wrekin, the Long Mynd and the Malvern Hills are all clearly visible.

Holehouse Farm. Follow the footpath NW until you reach a lane, then walk along the lane in the same direction until you reach the minor road at **Gorseybank**. Go left down the road and, where it forks, follow the road to the **rail crossing**. At the other side of the crossing take the next road junction right and follow this until it ends at a lane. Bear left and follow the lane along the side of sports fields to emerge back onto Coldwell Street, where you should turn left to return to Market Place in **Wirksworth**.

Moot Hall is where the Barmote Court sits in session to this day. Situated in Chapel Lane, the court presides over mining claims and is said to be the oldest industrial court in Britain. At the court sessions, lead is weighed against a standard brass dish dating back to the Tudor period. The proceedings are presided over by 12 residents from the High Peak area.

WALK 34

Tissington to Thorpe Cloud

Start/Finish	Tissington SK 177 521
Distance	6 miles (10km)
Ascent/Descent	335m
Time	3hr
Terrain	Minor roads, fields, trail. One steep ascent and descent
Map	OS 1:25000 Explorer OL24
Refreshments	Tissington
Parking	Tissington car park SK 177 521

There are not many 'peaks' in the Peak District, but Thorpe Cloud is one. It is well worth the climb for the views along Dovedale and the satisfaction of reaching the top. The walk takes you through this feudal landscape with its ridge and furrow crop system. The return journey winds its way through the village of Thorpe and its wonderful Norman church, before gently returning you to the medieval landscape around Tissington.

Thorpe Cloud, one of the few peaks in the Peak District

From the **Tissington Trail car park** turn left and follow the road into the centre of the village. Continue past the turning for **Tissington Hall** and cross the cattle grid, then walk up the road along a line of lime trees that are over 200 years old. On reaching the gates to **Tissington**, walk across the **A515** then down the road immediately opposite, until just before the road bends left in the bottom of the dip.

MEDIEVAL CULTIVATION

The land that surrounds Tissington is one of the finest examples of the medieval feudal field system of ridge and furrow cultivation, which was necessary to provide food for the community. Each household was allocated strips of land that they had to cultivate. Every year the land was divided equally across the villages so that no strip was cultivated by the same family in successive years. This ensured that everyone got a fair share of the good and the bad land. The ridge and furrows, much higher than they are today, were produced by ploughing with a single-sided ploughshare that placed the earth towards the centre of the ridge. The rows that curve towards the end show where the plough teams turned and indicate that these fields date from the system's earliest period. The fields survive today because sheep replaced crops in the 15th century and so the land was never ploughed again. The introduction of large numbers of sheep brought dewponds into the landscape as a means of collecting water for the flocks to drink.

Take the footpath stile hidden in the hedgerow on the left across the field diagonally left exiting via a squeeze stile onto the road. Go straight across the road and through the stile, then follow the footpath SW across a series of fields, using seven stiles or gates and ending on a narrow tarmac lane after a dewpond and just S of **Pike House**.

Go left and then right through the squeeze stile and follow the hedge line on the right down the field and through a gate. Walk a few metres on, then follow the footpath through the hedge on the right and continue downhill, now with the hedge on the left. Go through two gates at the bottom of the field and follow the footpath across open fields. ◄

Do not enter the rifle range area. If there are any red flags flying, they are warning that target practice is in operation.

Follow the left-hand wall past the rear of the **Peveril in the Peak Hotel**. Where the path meets a farm track in front of Thorpe Cloud go right and follow the path down through **Lin Dale** to the gate leading into **Dove Dale**. Go through the gate, then immediately left and follow the footpath that zigzags its way up to the summit of **Thorpe Cloud**.

Thorpe Cloud is a reef knoll created when the area was part of a tropical sea and the calcified remains of creatures formed the limestone rock you see today. The name 'cloud' stems from *clud*, meaning hill. The summit provides a wonderful panoramic view of the surrounding area and up the beautiful

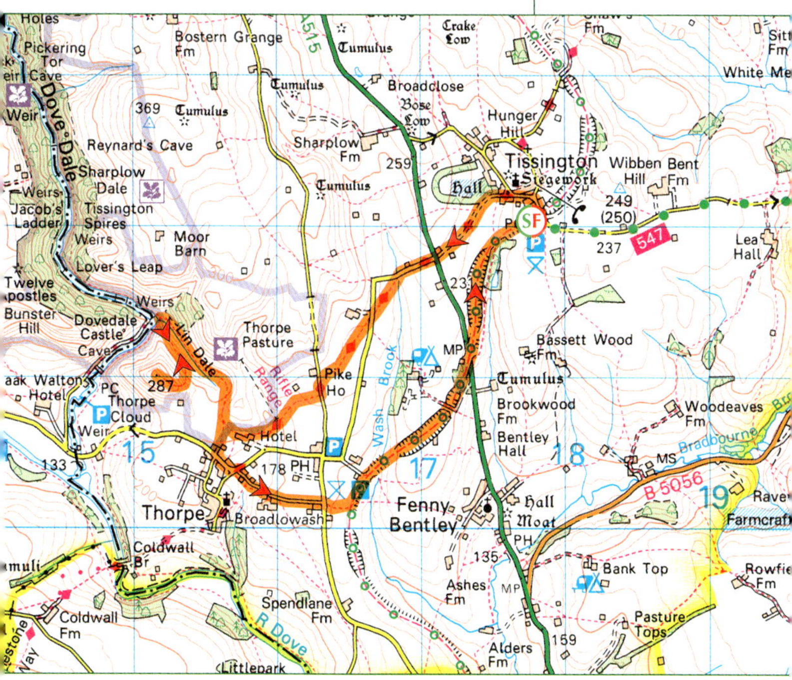

Dove Dale. One interesting feature discovered recently is that, around the summer solstice, a double sunset can be detected on the summit when viewed from the top of Lin Dale.

Retrace your steps to the farm track at the top of Lin Dale. At the track carry straight on to a gate. Go through and cross the road to enter **Thorpe**. Walk through the village to the church. ◀

Spend time in the churchyard reading a few of the epitaphs on the headstones; some offer excellent advice.

Take the lane to the left of the church, following it across a footbridge to a narrow road. Go right and walk up the road to a junction at **Broadlowash**. Go across the junction through a gate opposite and E across fields and two further gates, eventually arriving on the **Tissington Trail**. Go left and follow the trail back to **Tissington car park**.

WALK 35
Ashbourne to Thorpe

Start/Finish	Tissington Trail, Ashbourne SK 175 469
Distance	6 miles (10km)
Ascent/Descent	195m
Time	3hr
Terrain	Minor country roads, footpaths, trail
Map	OS 1:25000 Explorer OL24, 259 Derby
Refreshments	Tissington Trail, Ashbourne
Parking	Tissington Trail, Ashbourne SK 175 469

This is a wonderful half-day walk to the pretty village of Thorpe, within easy access of Ashbourne. The churches of St Oswald in Ashbourne, St Mary in Mapleton and St Leonard in Thorpe are of particular interest. The walk is a gentle stroll through an ancient landscape of rolling hills full of history. The view of Thorpe Cloud from Thorpe is very pleasing as is the return journey along the Tissington Trail.

ASHBOURNE

This is a beautiful town, where Church Street will be of particular interest to lovers of architecture. At one end sits the 16th-century Grammar School with lovely mullioned windows while, on the opposite side of the street, the 18th-century Italianate Mansion House provides a complete contrast. The church of St Oswald is deceptive. Its massive size is hidden from the eye by its siting in a valley. Inside, the chapels of the Bradbournes and the Cockaynes have wonderful alabaster effigies lying on ornate tombs. Around the church and towards the town centre are several almshouses, some set around pretty courtyards. Closer to the town centre is the Georgian Green Man Hotel, with its sign stretching all the way across the road. Both Boswell and Johnson stayed here on their travels around the country.

The Ashbourne Game (Royal Shrovetide Football) takes place each year on Shrove Tuesday and Ash Wednesday. The game involves a football being released in the centre of Ashbourne with goals at opposite ends of the town. If either of the two teams, the 'Up'Ards' or the 'Down'Ards, scores a goal the game is restarted. Any goal scorers are carried aloft to the Green Man Hotel courtyard for a celebratory drink!

Midway through the tunnel there is a frisson of excitement. I will not spoil the surprise.

The cycle hire centre at the start of the Tissington Trail can be accessed directly from the market town of **Ashbourne** by walking along the illuminated former railway tunnel, whose entrance is on Station Road in the centre of town. ◀

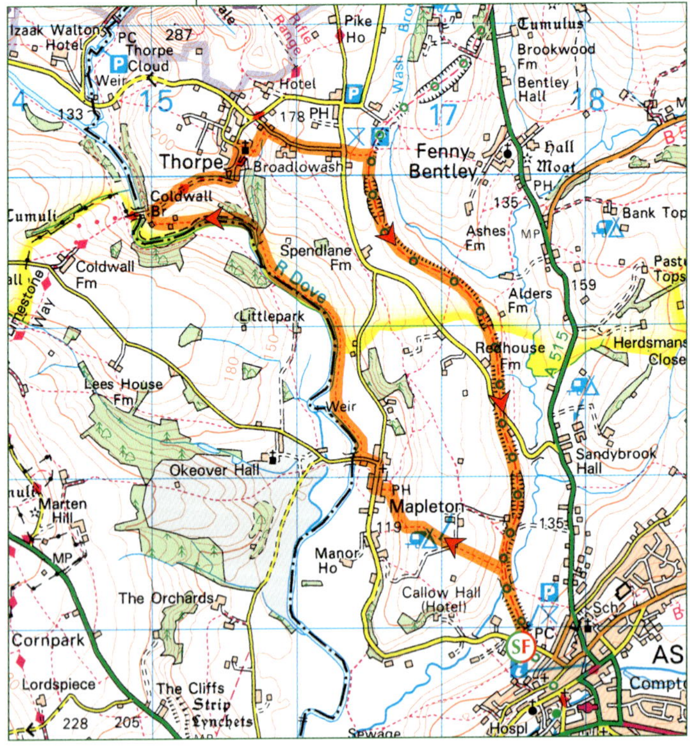

From the cycle hire centre in Mappleton Lane, join the **Tissington Trail** for approximately 500 metres, then descend the steps on the left giving access to a field.

Rise through two fields via stiles to a well-laid out camping area and walk NW over a tarmac drive. Follow the footpath between fence and hedge, eventually emerging via a stile into a field. Bear diagonally right then, just after going through a squeeze stile and gate, follow the footpath with a hedge to your right down to a gap between hedgerows. Turn right through the gap and gradually descend to the rear of **Mapleton church**.

The Church of St Mary at Mapleton designed by James Gibbs

James Gibbs, a protégé of Sir Christopher Wren, designed both St Martin-in-the-Fields in London and the domed Radcliffe Camera in Oxford. He was also the architect of the 18th-century Church of St Mary at Mapleton, with its octagonal domed lantern. He gave his name to a doorway surround – the Gibbs surround – that features a triangular pediment. Such a doorway can be seen in the nearby almshouses, known as the Okeover Clergy House.

Enter the churchyard and walk straight ahead onto the road. Turn right then left at the next junction towards **Mapleton Bridge**. Just before the bridge, take the footpath on your right and follow the **River Dove** upstream to **Coldwall Bridge**. Go right and walk up the wide, steep track.

Note the arrow-sharpening marks on the entrance porch, then seek out some of the humorous headstone inscriptions in the churchyard near the doorway.

Enter the village of **Thorpe**, stopping to admire the view of Thorpe Cloud and to explore the wonderful church of St Leonard's. ◀

Immediately after the church, take the narrow lane to your right and walk past the small gate leading into the church, then turn left down the side of a field boundary to emerge onto **Broadlowash Lane**. Walk up the hill to your right passing a farm on your right and go straight across at the junction into a field via a gate. Cross the small field to a second gate and then walk down the next field to a kissing gate leading onto the **Tissington Trail**. Go right along the trail to return to the cycle hire centre at **Ashbourne**.

The High Peak Trail (Walk 40)

WALK 36
Derwent Valley Heritage Way

Start	Grindleford Station SK 251 787
Finish	Ambergate SK 348 515
Distance	24 miles (38km)
Ascent	460m
Time	12hr
Terrain	Minor country roads, footpaths, trails
Map	OS 1:25000 Explorer OL24
Refreshments	Grindleford, Baslow, Matlock, Ambergate
Public transport	Buses available for Grindleford and Ambergate
Parking	Grindleford Station SK 251 787, Ambergate Station SK 348 515

The Derwent Valley Heritage Way (DVHW) is an excellent route to explore the eastern side of the White Peak. This section on the OS White Peak OL24 map covers the route between the rail stations at Grindleford and Ambergate (the full route is 51 miles/82km long and runs from Heatherdene to Derwent Mouth, near Shardlow). The walk follows the River Derwent along the valley floor making for easy walking with little ascent. Stretched out along the whole of the route are numerous places for rest and refreshment, suitable for a single-day challenge or a multi-day minibreak.

There are so many things to see on this walk. Hours could be spent on the riverbank watching kingfishers and rising trout or breathing in the heady fragrance of the wild garlic. A whole day can be lost at Chatsworth House looking at valuable art or exploring the exquisite grounds. For the historically minded, the World Heritage Site of Cromford Mills is a must. This, the world's first industrial factory complex, turned what was a cottage industry producing textiles into the Industrial Revolution. The walk alongside Cromford Canal, past the Leawood Pump House, is a delight in late spring and summer.

From **Grindleford Station** walk across the bridge and follow the wide track heading NW. Just after Padley Chapel, take the footpath on the left over the rail line and bear left where it forks to join the Derwent Valley Heritage

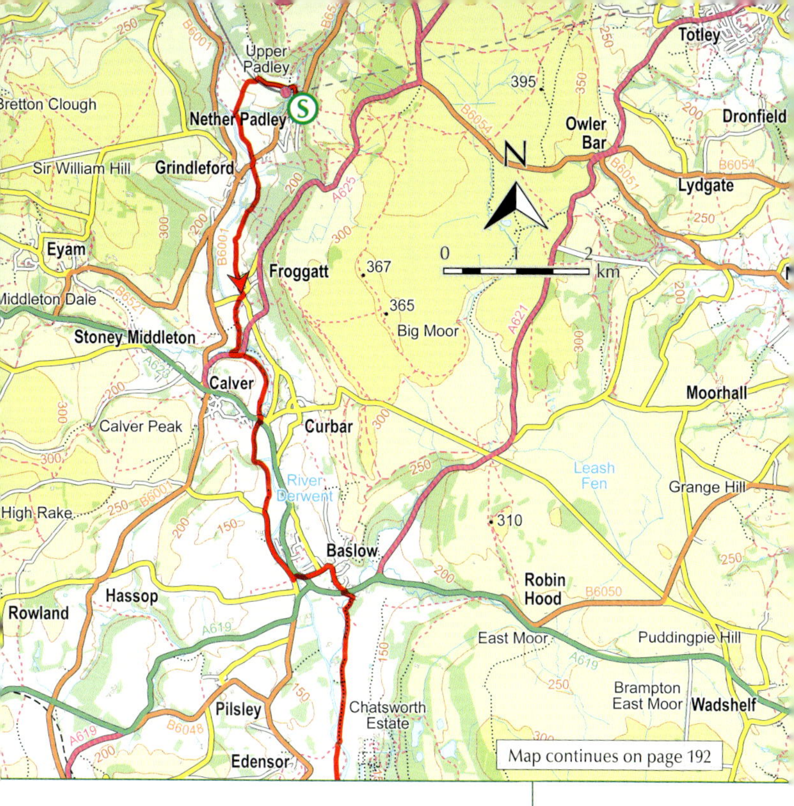

Way by the **River Derwent**. Turn left and head S following the river downstream. At the **B6521** cross the road diagonally right and enter a large field, then follow the footpath away from the river and through woodland on a paved path. Exit the woods and proceed across fields to **Froggatt**. Bear right where the road forks and take the footpath, just after crossing the bridge, to rejoin the river on the western bank. Keep to the footpath, always ensuring you are following the purple and yellow DVHW waymark until you arrive at **Baslow**.

Follow the road through the village and cross the **A619** by the pelican crossing, walking forward over a stone bridge then bearing right into the **Chatsworth Estate**. ▶ Walk S through the park and cross the bridge

Home of the Duke of Devonshire, Chatsworth is one of the foremost stately homes in Britain; the house and gardens are well worth a visit.

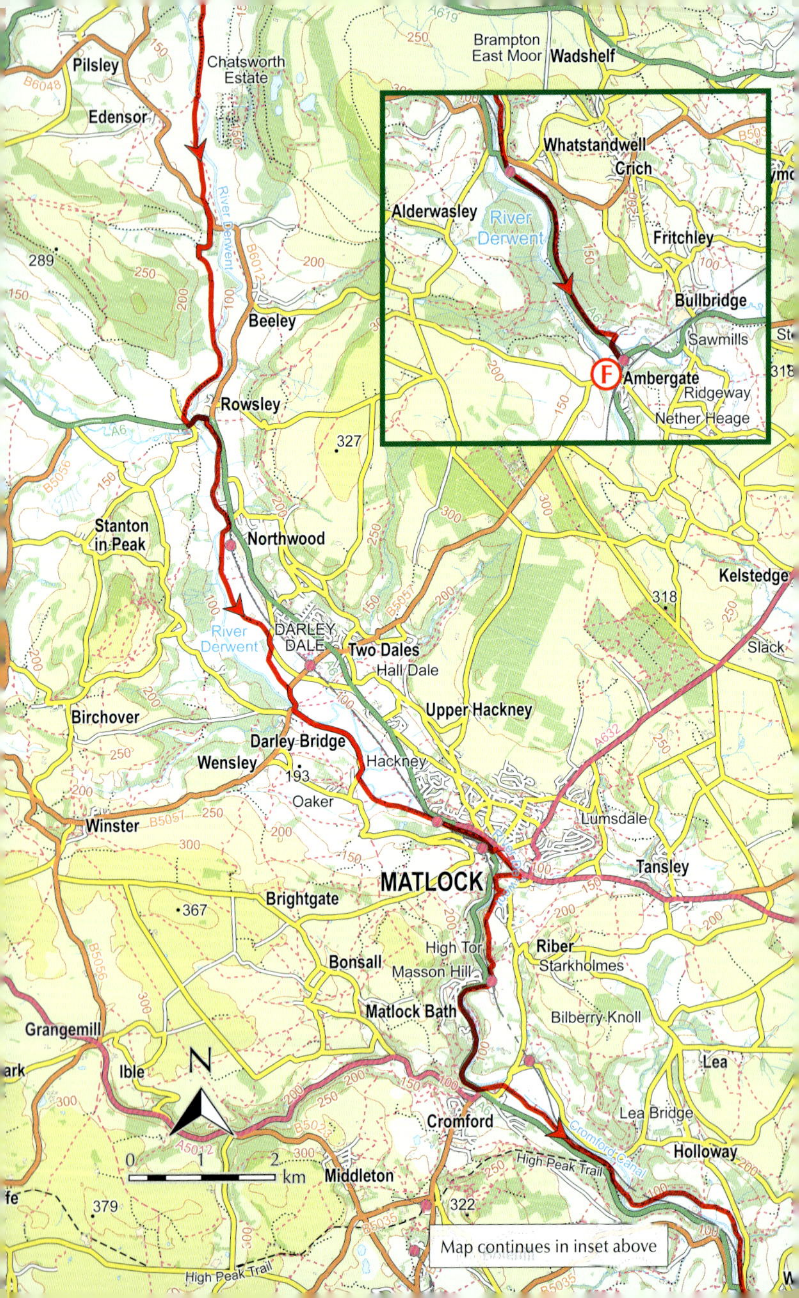

Pilsley
Edensor
Chatsworth Estate
Brampton East Moor
Wadshelf
Whatstandwell
Crich
Alderwasley
River Derwent
Fritchley
Bullbridge
Sawmills
Ambergate
F
Ridgeway
Nether Heage
Beeley
Rowsley
Stanton in Peak
Northwood
Kelstedge
Slack
River Derwent
DARLEY DALE
Two Dales
Hall Dale
Upper Hackney
Birchover
Darley Bridge
Hackney
Wensley
Oaker
Lumsdale
Winster
Tansley
MATLOCK
Brightgate
High Tor
Riber
Starkholmes
Bonsall
Masson Hill
Matlock Bath
Bilberry Knoll
Lea
Grangemill
Ible
Lea Bridge
Holloway
Cromford
Cromford Canal
High Peak Trail
Middleton
High Peak Trail
Map continues in inset above
N
0   1   2   km

by Queen Mary's Bower to continue along the western bank of the river. Cross the road by the cattle grid and walk to the right of the garden centre, following the lane to Calton Lees. Where the lane turns sharp right take the footpath straight ahead across fields, following the river downstream to **Rowsley**.

Go left along the **A6** and, just before a mini roundabout, take the footpath on the right along the disused rail line. Pass the Peak Rail line on your left and continue SE to **Darley Bridge**. Go right at the **B5057** and cross the bridge, then take the footpath left along the riverbank to Matlock Bridge. Go left across the packhorse bridge and, at the other side, turn right onto the footpath on the NE bank of the river. Follow this to the junction of three minor roads at **Matlock**, then go right and right again to rejoin the DVHW. Follow the route across the bridge into **Matlock Bath**. Continue along the road to the junction with Cromford and take the footpath left into **Cromford Mill**. ▶ Cross the road to Cromford Wharf and follow the Cromford Canal all the way to **Ambergate**.

The Cromford Canal at High Peak Junction

This is where British cotton production began on an industrial scale. It changed the way people work, moving from a farming-based economy to an industrial factory-based one.

193

WALK 37

Eastern Gritstone Trail

Start	Grindleford Station SK 251 787
Finish	Bakewell SK 217 684
Distance	23 miles (37km)
Ascent	1120m
Time	11hr
Terrain	Minor country roads, footpaths
Map	OS 1:25000 Explorer OL24
Refreshments	Grindleford, Baslow, Birchover, Bakewell
Public transport	Buses available for Grindleford Station and Bakewell
Parking	Grindleford SK 251 787, Bakewell SK 220 686

The Peak District is blessed with perhaps the finest gritstone edges in the country. They are a mecca for climbers and have hundreds of routes along their length. This walk links up edges forming the eastern boundary of the White Peak area. There are four edges in total, some long, some short. Interspersed with the edges are points of gritstone that are geologically, archeologically and culturally significant. On a clear day with the sun and blue skies above, the view looking out from the edges across the Peak to the western edge is something that is hard to beat.

Walking along the edges is like walking through ancient and modern history. On the moors there are many stone circles, cairns and settlements that date back to the Bronze Age. The gritstone was quarried for building stone and millstone and there's plenty of evidence still to be seen.

From Grindleford Station take the footpath to the right of the café, cross the road and ascend Oaks Wood until you arrive at stepping-stones. Cross the stream and follow the wall line on the right up the steep slope, then go through the gate into the woodland. Follow the footpath downhill until you emerge onto a tarmac lane. Go left and then left again along a footpath rising through woodland and heading due S, until you arrive at the **A625**.

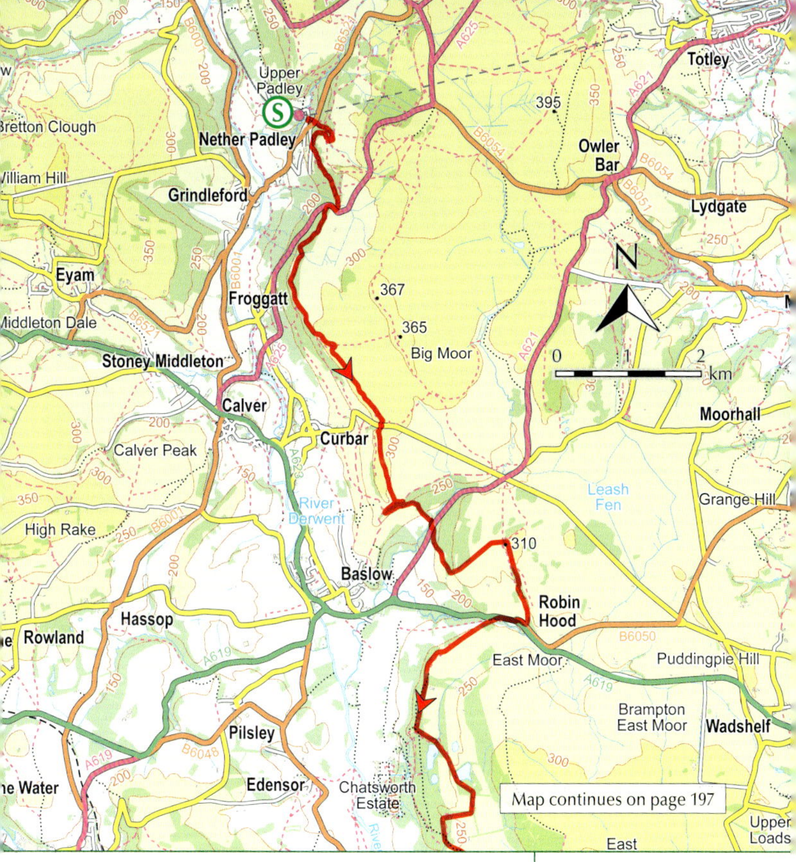

Cross diagonally to your right and go through the gate. Walk along **Froggatt Edge** and **Curbar Edge** then cross Curbar Gap road and continue along **Baslow Edge** until you reach the stone cross of Wellington's Monument. ▶

Go right down the track and, where a footpath leads off underneath Baslow Edge, go left and follow the footpath down through woodland to cross the **A621** into woods then uphill to three large cairns. Turn left and follow the wall line along to the foot of Birchen Edge. Ascend the rocky path below the triangulation pillar then turn right along the edge, at the end descending to the

Along the way you will pass over many of the climbing routes first conquered by the greats of British mountaineering and climbing, including pioneers Joe Brown and Don Whillans.

195

Froggatt Edge has been a climbing venue for decades with hundreds of routes along its length

track that leads to the **A619**. Go right, down the road, passing the pub on your right, then cross to the footpath leading into the **Chatsworth Estate**.

Cross the stream then bear right along the footpath leading to Dobb Edge. ◄ Continue walking SE over several stiles until you enter the forest above Chatsworth House. Follow the trail through the forest to the Hunting Tower then bear left to the Emperor Lake and Swiss Cottage, keeping on the trail until you exit the forest at a stone wall and walk along a grass trail across open moorland. Go through the gate at the end and go left along the track to the minor road. Take the concession footpath down through the woods then, just after clearing the trees, cross the road and follow the footpath down open fields then through woodland to end at a minor road leading to **Rowsley**. Cross the road and follow the footpath into the village. Cross the **River Derwent** and go left down a minor road that becomes a track. Pass through

Take care as the path passes close to the edge here.

Stanton Woodhouse and ascend the footpath through fields and woodland onto **Stanton Moor**.

Cross the moor heading SW to the road into **Birchover**. Follow the footpath down into the village and turn right down the lane to the **B5056**. Go left along the road then cross to ascend to **Robin Hood's Stride**. Cross the fields after this rock outcrop and go through Harthill Moor Farm, keeping to the public right of way, and follow the **Limestone Way** to **Bradford Dale**. Go right down the dale to **Alport** and take the footpath going N up across fields into **Bakewell**.

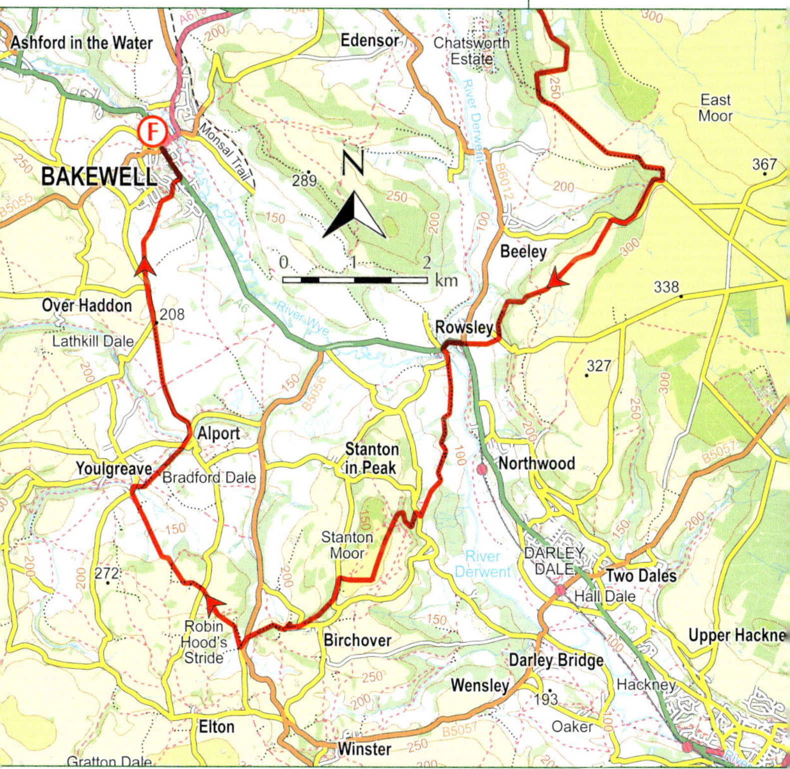

WALK 38

Limestone Way

Start	Monyash SK 149 665
Finish	Tissington SK 175 522
Distance	22 miles (35km)
Ascent	1025m
Time	11.5hr
Terrain	Minor country roads, footpaths, trails
Map	OS 1:25000 Explorer OL24
Refreshments	Monyash, Youlgreave, Parwich, Tissington
Public transport	Buses available for Monyash and Tissington
Parking	Monyash, Tissington

The Limestone Way stretches from Castleton to Rocester, a total distance of 46 miles (74km). The section covered by the eastern sheet of OL24 has perhaps the most beautiful scenery. It threads a way across the limestone plateau of the White Peak, dipping into idyllic dales lined with limestone crags that drip with plants and wildflowers. The sound of crystal-clear trout streams is a musical companion and in summer the dales provide welcome shade. Dotted along the route are some wonderful villages: Parwich is almost a chocolate-box picture, while the Tissington Estate takes you back to the feudal era. It is easy to spend more than a day on this stretch of the walk; midway is but a few miles from Matlock and all the delights that town holds. This is gentle walking and a good introduction to longer-distance walks. Short detours into the nearby villages can take you to some wonderful pubs for a welcome break.

This area is the centre of **lead mining** in the White Peak district of Wirksworth Hundred, an area of land similar to the wapentake lands, further north. Controlled by the laws laid down at the Barmote Court, a payment was extracted for the lead removed from the rich veins that ran through the limestone. Lead mining was present when the

Romans marched across these lands. The high point of production occurred in the 18th century but, by the middle of the 19th century, the industry had started to decline. Lead's traditional uses for roofing and piping began to be taken over by other materials. Today, lead is still mined along with other minerals, particularly fluorspar, under the ancient laws of the Barmote Court.

Head S from the village green at **Monyash**, following the road round until it takes a sharp right. Go straight on up the walled lane in a SE direction crossing the top of Fern Dale and carrying on to One Ash Grange Farm. Cross Cales Dale then keep to the left of Calling Low to pass through woodland before reaching a fork in a road. Take the right-hand fork through a car park into woodland and descend the hillside to a sharp bend in the road. Go right and across the road and take the footpath directly S to another road. Go right along the roadway and take the footpath on a hairpin bend SE down to the River Bradford. Cross the footbridge and follow the river downstream to a clapper bridge. Cross here and continue following the river down to a road. Go right along the road and take the footpath left into a field.

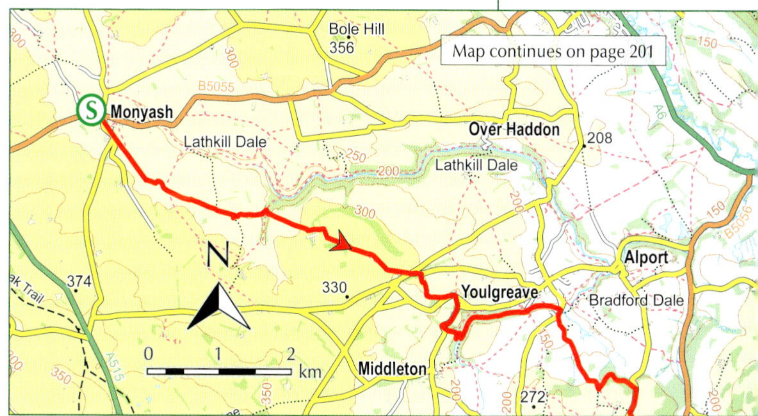

The old clapper bridge over the River Bradford

Follow the footpath uphill to a lane leading to Harthill Moor Farm and take the footpath left across a fence to enter woodland. Follow the path through the woods to a road. Turn right and take the footpath next left over to **Robin Hood's Stride**. Walk down to the road then take the narrow lane uphill past Dudwood Farm, emerging on the main road in **Elton**. Go straight across and follow the walled lane all the way to the outskirts of **Winster**.

Go left to the fork in the road and take the walled lane E, then head across fields in the same direction to a road leading into **Brightgate**. Cross Bonsall Moor until you reach a walled lane running NE. Turn left up the lane until you come to the crossing of paths and take the right-hand footpath to **Upper Town**. Follow the road down and at the junction turn right. After the hairpin bend, enter the small village square and take the footpath SW across fields, passing the disused Bonsall Mines on your left. Cross the road and maintain the same direction across numerous narrow fields to **Ible**. Follow the road right into **Grangemill**, taking the first footpath on the left along the edge of a quarry. Turn left and left again then, at the cross-roads, take the footpath S to intersect with another path running SE. Turn right along this route following it SW across the **High Peak Trail** to a road. Go right and right again along the road and take the footpath on the left in the third field, to join a walled lane that becomes a minor

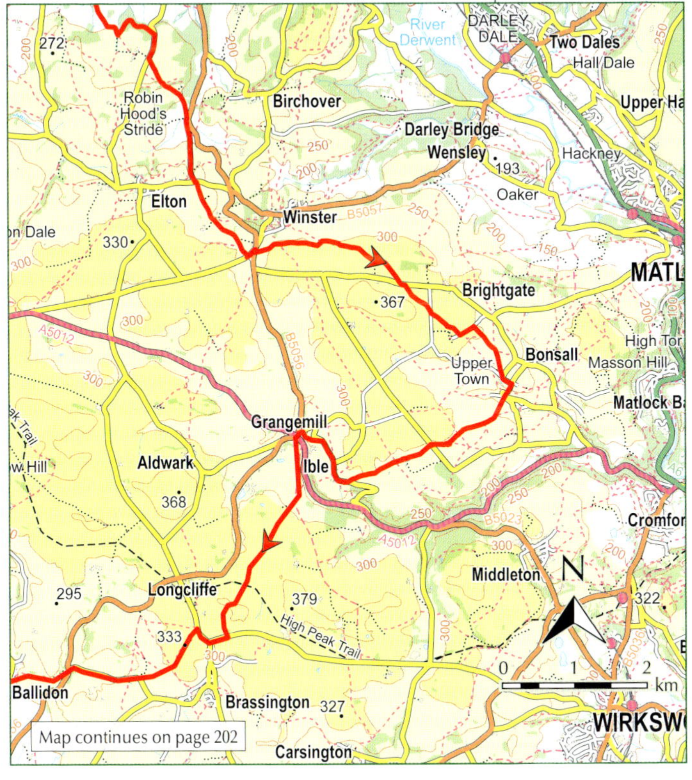

Map continues on page 202

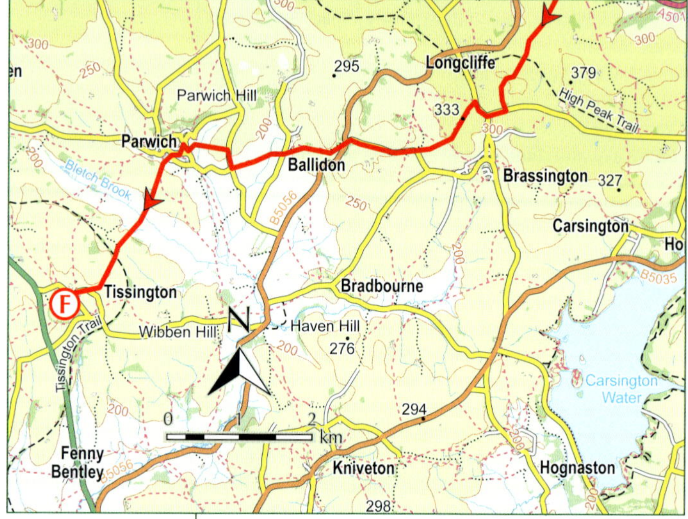

road heading due W. At the junction go straight across and follow the footpath over the road into **Ballidon**, then carry on SW to the road E of **Parwich**. Turn right then take the next footpath left across fields into the village.

Go W through the village and, after passing the church, go left along the green, passing a row of cottages. Take the footpath SW across **Bletch Brook** then ascend a hill to the **Tissington Trail**. Cross the trail and take the narrow country lane into **Tissington village**. Turn left at the junction to walk past Tissington Hall.

WALK 39

White Peak Circular

Start/Finish	Birchover SK 236 621
Distance	42 miles (70km). Day 1: 16 miles (26km), Day 2: 15 miles (25km), Day 3: 11 miles (19km)
Ascent	1570m. Day 1: 700m, Day 2: 440m, Day 3: 430m
Time	3 days. Day 1: 7.5hr, Day 2: 7hr, Day 3: 5.5hr
Terrain	Minor country roads, footpaths, trails
Map	OS 1:25000 Explorer OL24
Refreshments	Birchover, Biggin, Youlgreave, Monyash, Bakewell,
Parking	Birchover
Accommodation	Birchover, Biggin, Monyash

This multi-day walk around the eastern section of the White Peak limestone plateau makes for a wonderful long weekend in summer. Each day ends at a pub; what more could you want? Along the way you'll visit some beautiful White Peak villages and encounter some of the best scenery in the region.

The walk starts in Birchover, the centre of local druid activity. There is a sense of the long distant pass all the way along this route. Stone circles and Neolithic burial sites abound on lonely hilltops. This is a walk to take at your leisure and savour the landscape.

The villages that lie on or near the walk make for fine stopping-off or accommodation points. All have a variety of accommodation types from camping to B&B, hostels, pubs and hotel. Transport between the villages can be difficult so if you want to use the route as a series of daily walks, two cars may be useful. Bakewell is the main market town in Derbyshire and is a thriving, vibrant place. On Monday – market day – the town is thronged with visitors and stalls. Pubs abound on the route. They make for a pleasant interlude and are perhaps one of the walk's big attractions. Real ale is the Inn thing here, along with some excellent food. Four of the pubs are not to be missed: The Druid Inn at Birchover, Waterloo Inn at Biggin, Bull's Head at Monyash and Rutland Hotel in Bakewell.

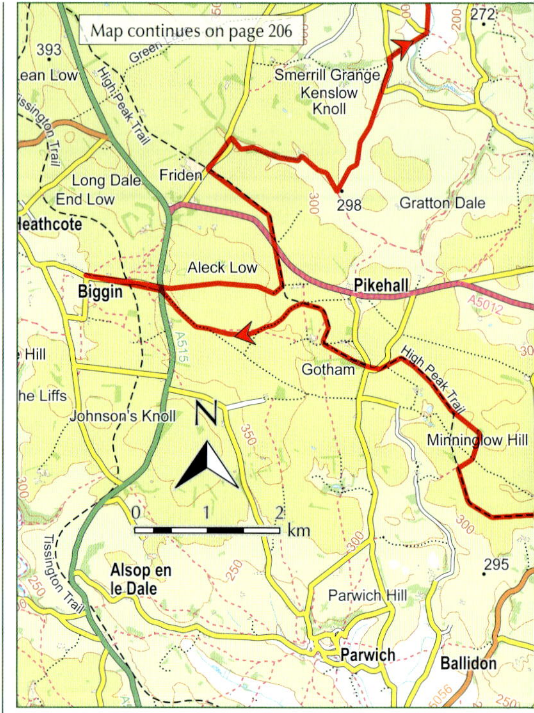

Day 1

Distance: 16 miles (26km), ascent: 700m, time: 7.5hr

From the Druid Inn in **Birchover**, walk E along Main Street and take the footpath on the right, just after the village pinfold, onto farmland. Cross several fields SE until you meet a footpath running directly S, following the line of a wall. Go right here and at the field boundary go across a walled lane. Head directly S to descend a footpath through a small wood out into open fields. Bear left at the junction of two paths and descend into a small valley, then climb up the other side and enter **Winster**.

Turn left through the village then right at the National Trust Market House and follow the road uphill

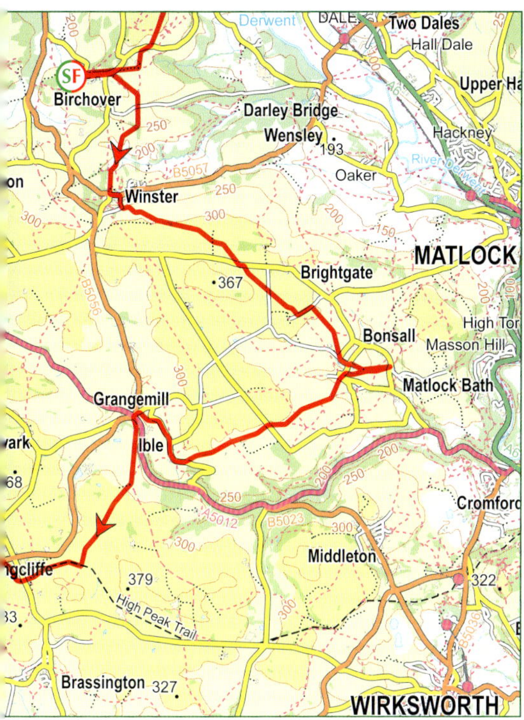

until it turns sharp right. Take the **Limestone Way** footpath SE across fields to Upper Town and then on to **Bonsall**. After visiting the Kings Head, retrace your steps to Upper Town and follow the Limestone Way past the Bonsall Mines to **Ible**. Turn right along the road and follow the trail to **Grangemill**. At the crossroads take the footpath S to the **Midshires Way/High Peak Trail** then go right along the trail. After passing **Gotham** leave the trail where it meets the lane to Pikehall and follow the walled lane SW until you come to a footpath on the right. Go along the path W, then along a walled lane NW to the **A515**. Cross the road and walk down into the village of **Biggin**.

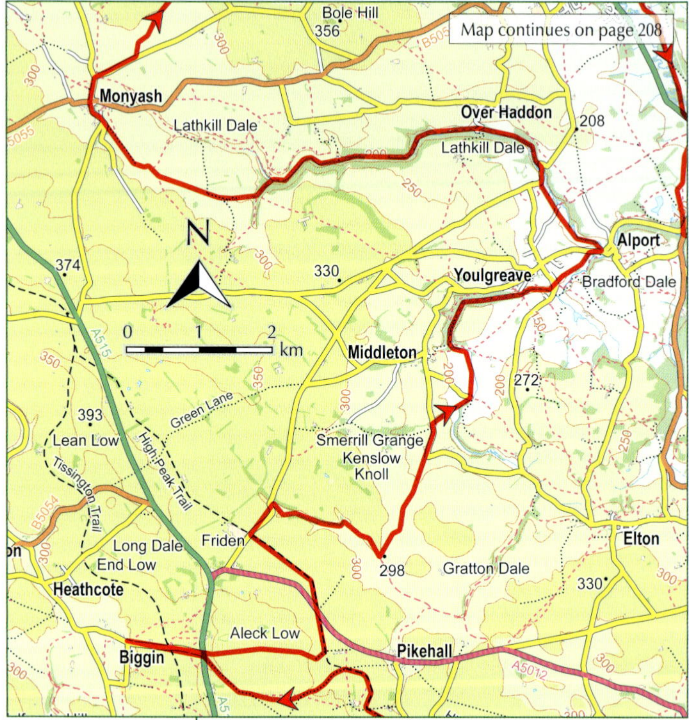

Day 2

Distance: 15 miles (25km), ascent: 440m, time: 7hr

Retrace your steps to the A515, then cross to the left of
houses and take the footpath E to the High Peak Trail.
Turn left along the trail then right along the minor road
from Friden, turning right into Long Dale shortly after. As
the dale deepens, ascend the left-hand slope to a gate
leading onto a bridleway heading almost NE towards
Smerrill Grange. Follow the bridleway to exit onto a road.
Turn left and take the second footpath on the right to
the end of a minor road. Cross the road and then fields,
keeping to the left of a tumbled-down barn, to reach the
Clapper Bridge over the River Bradford. Follow the river

downstream, crossing a second bridge below **Youlgreave** and then a road, and continue along the wide track to **Alport**.

Cross the road at Alport and follow the River Lathkill NW, upstream into **Lathkill Dale**. Just before a wooden footbridge, turn left up Cales Dale following the path right to One Ash Grange Farm. Follow the Limestone Way NW across the entrance to Fern Dale and enter a walled lane that takes you into **Monyash**.

Day 3

Distance: 11 miles (19km), ascent: 430m, time: 5.5hr
From the village cross go N along the road then take the right fork and the first footpath left, NE, across fields. Turn right along a minor road and, after a junction, take the footpath left to **Magpie Mine**.

The walled lane to Magpie Mine

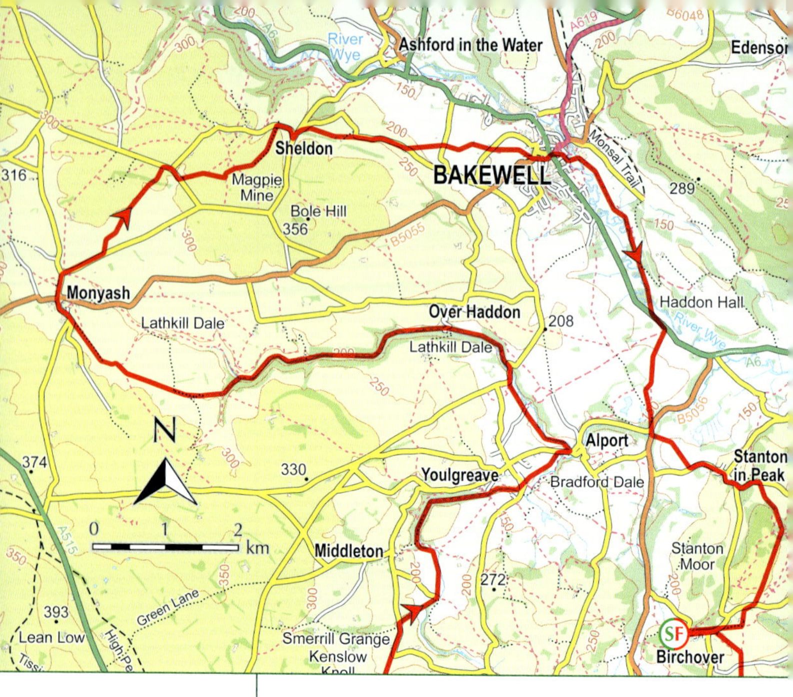

Take the footpath NE to the outskirts of **Sheldon**. Go right along the road and left at the junction and take the footpath E through Dirtlow Farm to a minor road. Carry on along the road, then take the next footpath on the left, E, across fields and minor roads to **Bakewell**.

Walk through Bakewell Market and across the footbridge, then along the eastern bank of the **River Wye**, SE to **Haddon Hall**. Cross the **A6** and ascend the hillside S, then descend to the junction of two minor roads. Carry on S, then take the first footpath on the left, E, to a narrow lane. Leave the lane and take the footpath SE to Stanton Hall. At the road go left uphill until you are clear of the village, then go right through trees to explore **Stanton Moor**. Use the footpath heading SW over the centre of the moor as a guide while exploring. Descend to the road into **Birchover**, then cross and follow the footpath S then W to the campsite. Turn left along the road to retrace your steps to the Druid Inn.

There are three easygoing trails that run through the eastern area of the White Peak. Each trail has its own character and explores different aspects of the area. The trails can be busy during holiday periods and, at peak times, can make for a less than pleasant experience as they cater for cyclists and horse riders as well as walkers. However, in quiet periods they provide a restful walk without having to worry about navigation. One big advantage of the trails is that they can be used as access points to other walks and, indeed, can be used to join two or more walks together. The trails have all been reclaimed from former rail lines, making them excellent surfaces for anyone who is, perhaps, less confident on rougher ground. Over the years, amenities have built up along the trails and you can now find café bars, cycle hire centres and bookshops. Although the routes along the trails have been planned from one end, they can be followed in either direction.

Scabious blanketing a track side verge

WALK 40

High Peak Trail

Start	Parsley Hay SK 146 638
Finish	High Peak Junction, Cromford SK 313 559
Distance	14.5 miles (23km)
Ascent	180m
Time	6hr
Terrain	Trail
Map	OS 1:25000 Explorer OL24
Refreshments	Parsley Hay, Middleton Top, Cromford
Public transport	Buses available for Parsley Hay and Cromford
Parking	Parsley Hay SK 146 638, Middleton Top SK 277 551, Cromford SK 314 560

The High Peak Trail is very unusual for a former railway line. The trail rises almost 305 metres across the top of the High Peak plateau between the car park at Parsley Hay, south of Buxton, and Cromford. The area's industrial heritage is much in evidence along the trail. Old quarry and mine workings line the sides with huge stone embankments carrying the line across deep dales. At Cromford, the line meets the World Heritage Site of the Derwent Valley Mills and Sir Richard Arkwright's factories, railway and canal. The steep incline between Cromford and Middleton Top, one of eight along the line, meant that wagons travelling north had to be pulled up by a steam engine. Today the engine runs for the delight of visitors, children of all ages.

From **Parsley Hay**, where cycle hire and refreshments are on offer, leave the visitor centre and head south along the trail. Where it splits you should take the left-hand fork maintaining a SE direction. Take care when crossing the **A515**. After crossing the minor road SE of **Gotham**, the trail passes the Neolithic site of **Minninglow** on the left-hand horizon. ◄

Minninglow is worth a short detour to inspect the burial chambers and cairns.

Back on the trail you will notice some old quarry workings and machinery that was used to build the

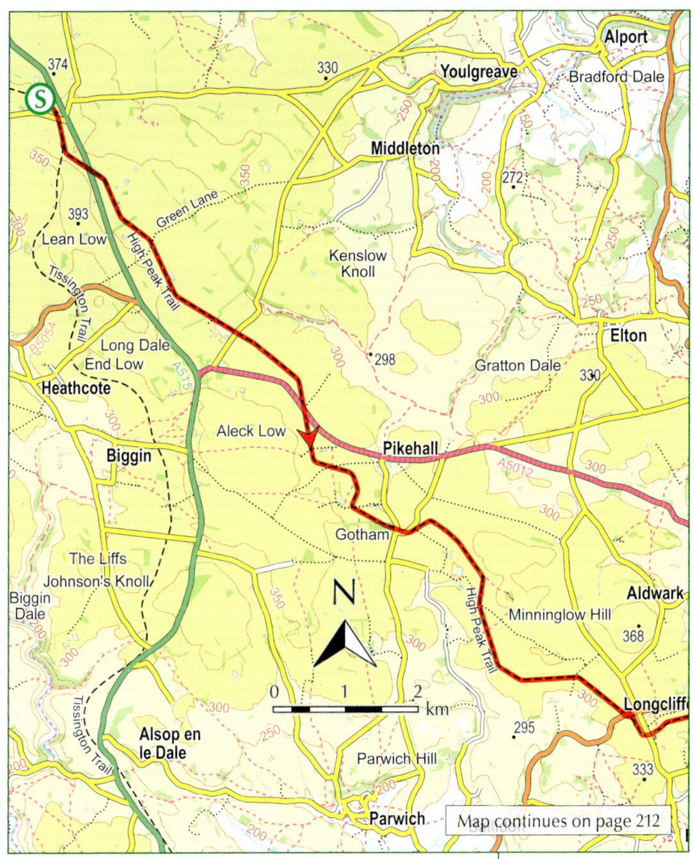

massive embankment you are standing on. You then come to a section of the trail that is especially fascinating for people interested in railway ephemera. Railway cottages, signs and buildings line the trail and bring you to **Middleton Top**, where you can see the Newcomen Engine. ▶ Carrying on, the trail passes the National Stone Centre, where you can view examples of Derbyshire stone, among many others. You can also explore the art

On certain days of the year you can watch the Newcomen Engine in action.

High Peak Junction on the Cromford Canal

If walking the trail from south to north, the incline to Middleton Top engine house is a good way of getting the blood pumping.

of drystone walling. Shortly after, keen climbers should definitely make a short detour to visit **Black Rock**. The trail then descends to the **High Peak Junction** at Cromford, meeting both the rail and canal that serviced the Cromford Mill. ◄

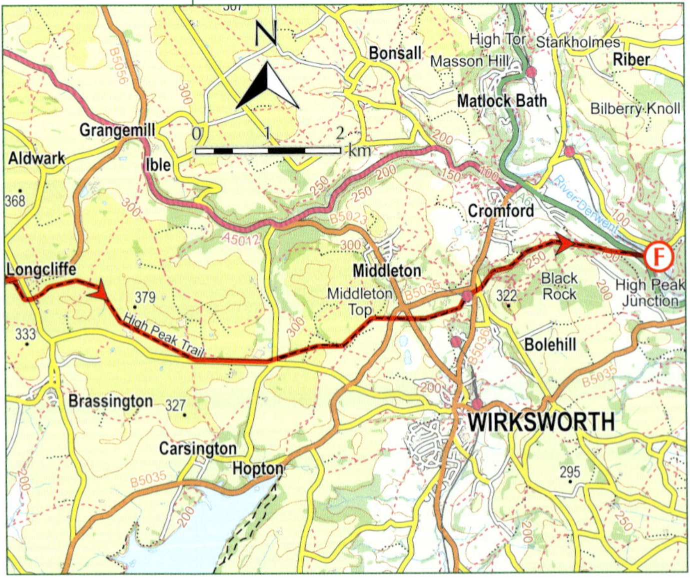

WALK 41

Tissington Trail

Start	Parsley Hay SK 146 638
Finish	Ashbourne SK 178 464
Distance	13 miles (21km)
Ascent	280m
Time	7hr
Terrain	Trail
Map	OS 1:25000 Explorer OL24
Refreshments	Parsley Hay, Hartington, Tissington, Ashbourne
Public transport	Buses available for Parsley Hay and Ashbourne
Parking	Parsley Hay SK 146 638, Hartington, Tissington, Ashbourne

The Tissington Trail landscape experience is very different to that of the High Peak Trail. This is a farming landscape of green pastures and small villages. The rail line was built to take milk and later stone to the industrial centres. It's easy to imagine the pastoral life enjoyed by those who worked and lived here. Along the trail there is again much to see. Railway enthusiasts will be delighted, as will historians who are interested in medieval England.

The village pond at Tissington complete with ducks

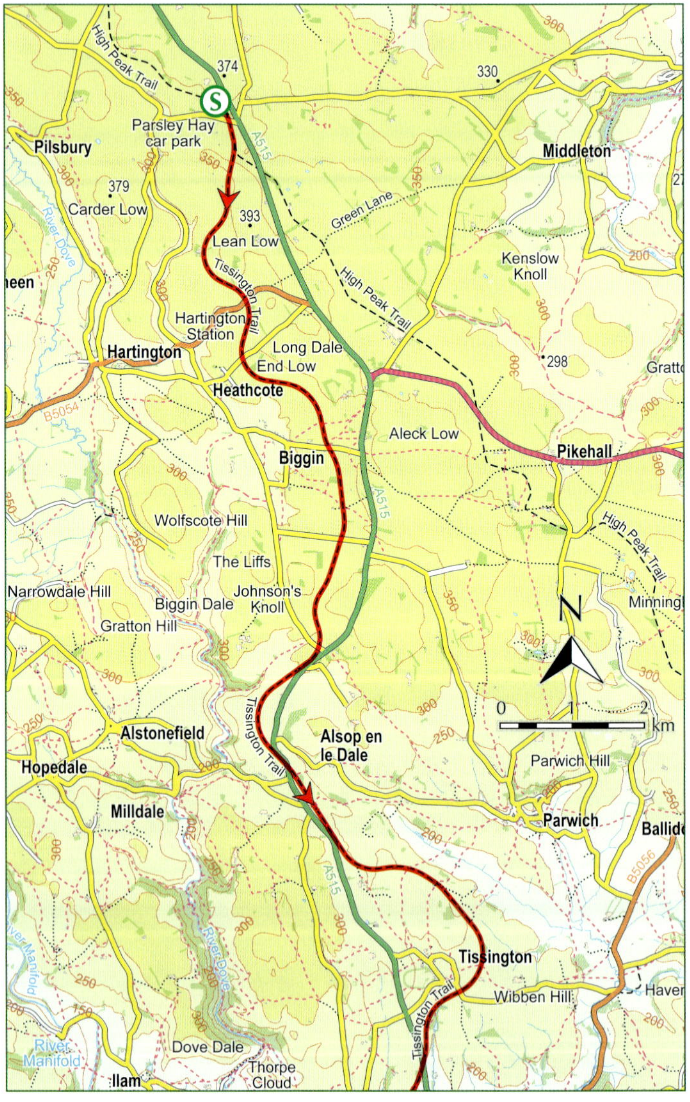
High Peak Trail
374
330
Pilsbury
Middleton
Parsley Hay car park
S
350
379
Carder Low
393
Lean Low
Green Lane
Kenslow Knoll
Tissington Trail
High Peak Trail
heen
Hartington Station
Long Dale
End Low
298
Hartington
Gratt
Heathcote
B5054
Aleck Low
Pikehall
Biggin
Wolfscote Hill
High Peak Trail
The Liffs
Narrowdale Hill
Johnson's Knoll
Minning
Biggin Dale
Gratton Hill
N
Tissington Trail
Alstonefield
Alsop en le Dale
0   1   2 km
Parwich Hill
Hopedale
Milldale
Parwich
Ballid
B5056
River Manifold
Tissington
Wibben Hill
Haver
River Manifold
River Dove
Dove Dale
Thorpe Cloud
Tissington Trail
Ilam

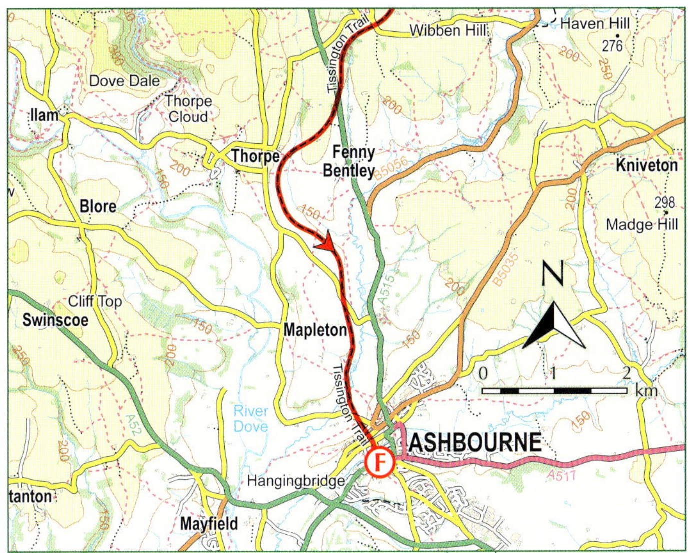

The trail starts at **Parsley Hay** running S to the famous **Hartington Station** signal box. Go in and imagine life as a signalman in the age of steam. ▶ From there the trail continues S, passing through the beautiful limestone-walled pastures of the White Peak until it arrives at the medieval estate village of **Tissington**. With a duck pond and green, a medieval house and Norman church, it feels like stepping back in time. There is an excellent café in the village as well as one by the trail. ▶

The trail continues to wind its way S with views of Thorpe Cloud, before entering the long tunnel that leads you to the end in **Ashbourne**.

The village of Hartington is close by and has wealth of places to visit.

The duck pond at Tissington provides a welcome place to spend a few minutes resting from the trail.

215

WALK 42
Monsal Trail

Start	Bakewell SK 230 678
Finish	Blackwell Mill SK 112 726
Distance	9.5 miles (15km)
Ascent	570m
Time	5hr
Terrain	Trail
Map	OS 1:25000 Explorer OL24
Refreshments	Bakewell, Hassop Station, Monsal Head, Miller's Dale
Public transport	Buses available for Bakewell and Blackwell
Parking	Bakewell SK 220 686, Hassop Station SK 217 705, Monsal Head SK 184 714, Miller's Dale SK 138 732, Wye Dale SK 112 724

The Monsal Trail is perhaps the most famous of the White Peak trails and it certainly receives the highest number of visitors. Its easy access and proximity to the major centres make it a magnet for families wanting a gentle and enjoyable day out. At peak times it can be very busy. The experience it offers is different to that of the other trails. Often the route is hidden away in a cutting, suddenly to emerge into a beautiful landscape, as though sitting on a train and looking out. But it also has tunnels. A pure delight for children, the tunnels are illuminated making for a very ethereal experience. And then there is the Headstone Viaduct, a marvel of engineering, fantastic views and a place to stand and ponder. Combine all this with some excellent refreshment stops and you can have a wonderful family day out.

From the visitor information centre in **Bakewell** head NE over the packhorse bridge then take Coombs Road SE 1 mile (1.5km) to the start of the trail. The trail runs N past Bakewell until it reaches **Hassop Station** where you will find a café, a bookshop and cycle hire. The trail then turns NE, past Thornbridge Hall, to enter the Headstone

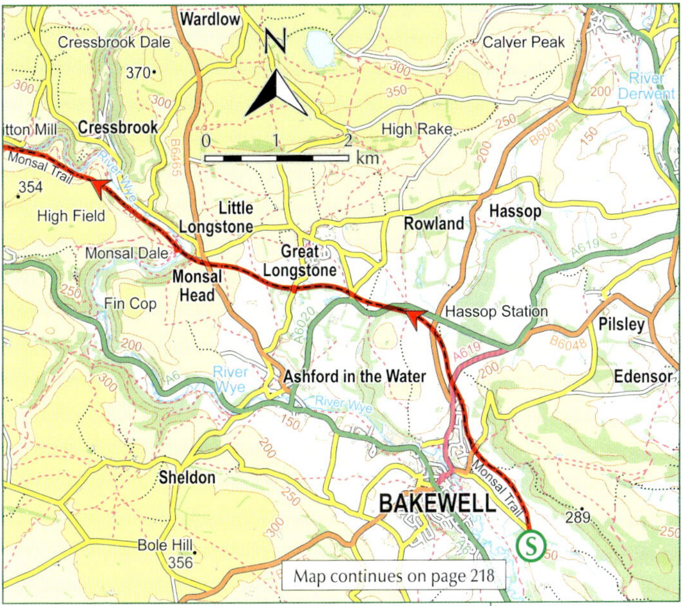

Map continues on page 218

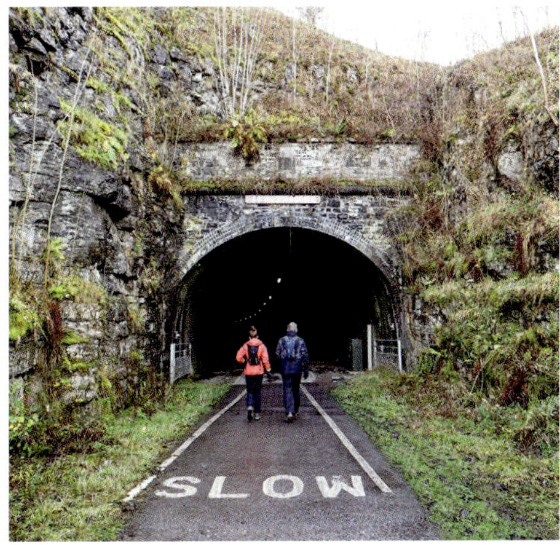

Walking along the Monsal Trail is easier now that the tunnels have been opened

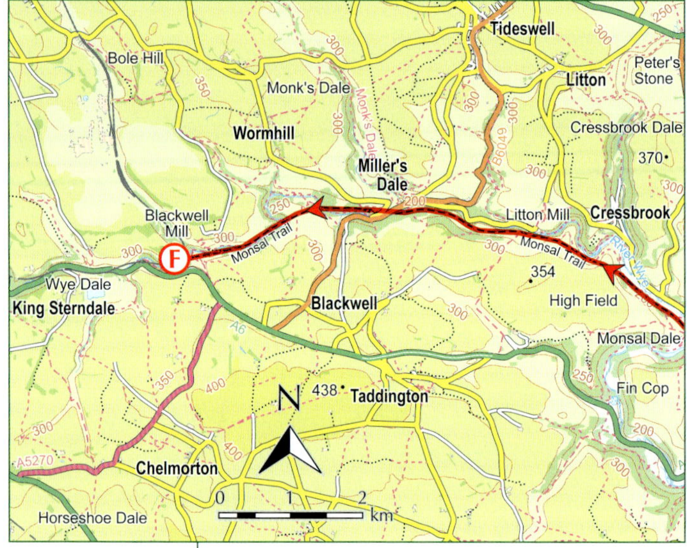

The Monsal Trail tunnels bring a new experience to walking. Children love the echoes that bounce around the walls.

Tunnel that decants you onto the Headstone Viaduct at **Monsal Head**.

Above the trail to the right are the Monsal Head Hotel and a coffee shop. Continue across the viaduct and pass through the **Cressbrook** and **Litton** tunnels. ◄ After passing the limekilns you come to **Miller's Dale** where the station has recently been refurbished to provide better facilities. Finally, the Chee Tor tunnels bring you to the cycle hire point at **Blackwell Mill**.

APPENDIX A
Route summary table

Walk		Start/Finish	Distance	Time	Page
Northern section					
1	Bradwell to Offerton	Bradwell	12 miles (19km)	6hr	31
2	Hope to Shatton	Hope	5.5 miles (9km)	3hr	37
3	Longshaw to Curbar Gap	Longshaw Estate	10 miles (16km)	5hr	41
4	Grindleford to White Edge	Grindleford Station	8.5 miles (14km)	4.5hr	46
5	Foolow to Wardlow	Foolow	7 miles (11.5km)	4hr	51
6	Eyam to Abney	Eyam	10 miles (16km)	5hr	54
7	Eyam to Grindleford	Eyam	11 miles (17.5km)	5.5hr	59
8	Eyam Village	Eyam	5.5 miles (9km)	3hr	63
9	Tideswell to Cressbrook	Tideswell	6 miles (10km)	3hr	68
10	Curbar to Gardoms Edge	Curbar Gap	7.5 miles (12km)	4.5hr	72
11	Calver to Hassop	Calver	8 miles (12.5km)	4.5hr	77
12	Calver to Great Longstone	Calver	8 miles (13km)	4.5hr	81
13	Taddington to Monsal Dale	Taddington	7 miles (11.5km)	4hr	85
14	Chatsworth to Beeley	Chatsworth House	8 miles (12.5km)	4.5hr	88
15	Ashford in the Water to Monsal Head	Ashford in the Water	7 miles (11.5km)	4hr	92

Walk		Start/Finish	Distance	Time	Page
16	Bakewell to Chatsworth	Bakewell	9.5 miles (15.5km)	5hr	97
17	Bakewell to Monsal Head	Bakewell	8.5 miles (14km)	4.5hr	102
18	Bakewell to Over Haddon	Bakewell	7.5 miles (12km)	4.5hr	106
19	Monyash to Sheldon	Monyash	8.5 miles (14km)	4.5hr	111
20	Rowsley to Birchover	Rowsley	9 miles (14.5km)	4.5hr	114
Southern section					
21	Youlgreave to Elton	Youlgreave	6 miles (10km)	3hr	121
22	Middleton to Elton	Middleton	9 miles (14.5km)	4.5hr	126
23	Middleton to Kenslow Knoll	Middleton	4 miles (6.5km)	2hr	131
24	Winster to Bonsall	Winster	8 miles (13km)	4.5hr	135
25	Matlock to Dethick	Matlock	7 miles (11.5km)	4hr	140
26	Biggin to Minninglow	Biggin	10 miles (16km)	5hr	145
27	Cromford to Black Rock	Cromford	5 miles (8km)	3hr	151
28	Cromford to Crich	Cromford	8.5 miles (14km)	4.5hr	155
29	Middleton to Harboro Rocks	Middleton Top	7 miles (12km)	4.5hr	158
30	Brassington to Kniveton	Brassington	11 miles (18km)	6hr	162
31	Parwich to Alsop en le Dale	Parwich	5.5 miles (9km)	3hr	168
32	Parwich to Tissington	Parwich	6.5 miles (10.5km)	3.5hr	171

Walk		Start/Finish	Distance	Time	Page
33	Wirksworth to Alport Height	Wirksworth	9 miles (14.5km)	4.5hr	175
34	Tissington to Thorpe Cloud	Tissington	6 miles (10km)	3hr	181
35	Ashbourne to Thorpe	Tissington Trail	6 miles (10km)	3hr	185
Long walks and trails					
36	Derwent Valley Heritage Way	Grindleford Station/ Ambergate	24 miles (38km)	12hr	190
37	Eastern Gritstone Trail	Grindleford Station/Bakewell	23 miles (37km)	12hr	194
38	Limestone Way	Monyash/ Tissington	22 miles (35km)	11.5hr	198
39	White Peak Circular	Birchover	42 miles (70km) 16 miles (26km), 15 miles (25km), 11 miles (19km)	3 days. 7.5hr, 7hr, 5.5hr	203
40	High Peak Trail	Parsley Hay / Cromford	14.5 miles (23km)	6hr	210
41	Tissington Trail	Parsley Hay/ Ashbourne	13 miles (21km)	7hr	213
42	Monsal Trail	Bakewell/ Blackwell	9.5 miles (15km)	5hr	216

APPENDIX B
Useful websites

Access
www.openaccess.naturalengland.org.uk

Accommodation
https://www.visitpeakdistrict.com/
accommodation

British Mountaineering Council
www.thebmc.co.uk

Eastern Moors Partnership
www.visit-eastern-moors.org.uk

Moors for the Future
www.moorsforthefuture.org.uk

National Trust
www.nationaltrust.org.uk/features/
high-peak-moors-derbyshire

Peak District National Park
www.peakdistrict.gov.uk

Peak District National Park Visitor
Centre
The Old Market
Bridge Street
Bakewell
DE45 1DS
tel 01629 813227
https://www.peakdistrict.gov.uk/visiting/
visitor-centres/bakewell

Royal Society for the Protection of Birds
www.rspb.org.uk

The Wildlife Trusts
www.wildlifetrusts.org

Transport
www.peakdistrict.gov.uk/visiting/
publictransport

Well Dressings
www.visitpeakdistrict.com/whats-on/
well-dressings

White Peak Walking
paulbesley.blog

YHA
www.yha.org.uk

APPENDIX C
Bibliography and further reading

Arts in the Peak (2019). *Companion stones*. Retrieved from www.companionstones.
org.uk/home/home1.htm

Bellamy, R (1981). *The Peak District Companion*. London, David and Charles.

Boatman, D (1982). *The natural history of Britain and Northern Europe. Fields and Lowlands*. London, Hodder and Stoughton Limited.

Edwards, KC, Swinnerton, HH, Hall, RH (1973). *The Peak District*. Glasgow, Collins.

Evans, P (2018). *How to see nature*. London, Batsford.

Goodwin, M (2019). *Rock as Gloss*. Sheffield, Longbarrow Press.

Parish of Middleton and Smerril (2019). *Sites of Meaning*. Retrieved from www.
sitesofmeaning.org.uk

Pevsner, N (1953). *The buildings of England. Derbyshire*. London, Penguin Books Limited.

Nine Stone Close, Harthill Moor (Walk 22)

DOWNLOAD THE ROUTES
IN GPX FORMAT

All the routes in this guide are available for download from:

www.cicerone.co.uk/976/GPX

as standard format GPX files. You should be able to load them into most online GPX systems and mobile devices, whether GPS or smartphone. You may need to convert the file into your preferred format using a conversion programme such as gpsvisualizer.com or one of the many other such websites and programmes.

When you follow this link, you will be asked for your email address and where you purchased the guidebook, and have the option to subscribe to the Cicerone e-newsletter.

www.cicerone.co.uk

NOTES

NOTES

NOTES

NOTES

LISTING OF CICERONE GUIDES

BRITISH ISLES CHALLENGES, COLLECTIONS AND ACTIVITIES

Cycling Land's End to John o' Groats
The Big Rounds
The Book of the Bivvy
The Book of the Bothy
The Mountains of England & Wales:
  Vol 1 Wales
  Vol 2 England
The National Trails
Walking The End to End Trail

SCOTLAND

Ben Nevis and Glen Coe
Cycle Touring in Northern Scotland
Cycling in the Hebrides
Great Mountain Days in Scotland
Mountain Biking in Southern and
  Central Scotland
Mountain Biking in West and North
  West Scotland
Not the West Highland Way
Scotland
Scotland's Best Small Mountains
Scotland's Mountain Ridges
Skye's Cuillin Ridge Traverse
The Borders Abbeys Way
The Great Glen Way
The Great Glen Way Map Booklet
The Hebridean Way
The Hebrides
The Isle of Mull
The Isle of Skye
The Skye Trail
The Southern Upland Way
The Speyside Way
The Speyside Way Map Booklet
The West Highland Way
The West Highland Way
  Map Booklet
Walking Ben Lawers, Rannoch
  and Atholl
Walking in the Cairngorms
Walking in the Pentland Hills
Walking in the Scottish Borders
Walking in the Southern Uplands
Walking in Torridon
Walking Loch Lomond and
  the Trossachs
Walking on Arran
Walking on Harris and Lewis
Walking on Jura, Islay and Colonsay
Walking on Rum and the Small Isles
Walking on the Orkney and
  Shetland Isles
Walking on Uist and Barra
Walking the Cape Wrath Trail
Walking the Corbetts
  Vol 1 South of the Great Glen
  Vol 2 North of the Great Glen

Walking the Galloway Hills
Walking the Munros
  Vol 1 – Southern, Central and
  Western Highlands
  Vol 2 – Northern Highlands and
  the Cairngorms
Winter Climbs Ben Nevis and
  Glen Coe
Winter Climbs in the Cairngorms

NORTHERN ENGLAND ROUTES

Cycling the Reivers Route
Cycling the Way of the Roses
Hadrian's Cycleway
Hadrian's Wall Path
Hadrian's Wall Path Map Booklet
The C2C Cycle Route
The Pennine Way
The Pennine Way Map Booklet
The Coast to Coast Walk
The Coast to Coast Map Booklet
Walking the Dales Way
Walking the Dales Way Map Booklet

NORTH EAST ENGLAND, YORKSHIRE DALES AND PENNINES

Cycling in the Yorkshire Dales
Great Mountain Days in
  the Pennines
Mountain Biking in the
  Yorkshire Dales
St Oswald's Way and
  St Cuthbert's Way
The Cleveland Way and the
  Yorkshire Wolds Way
The Cleveland Way Map Booklet
The North York Moors
The Reivers Way
The Teesdale Way
Trail and Fell Running in the
  Yorkshire Dales
Walking in County Durham
Walking in Northumberland
Walking in the North Pennines
Walking in the Yorkshire Dales:
  North and East
Walking in the Yorkshire Dales:
  South and West

NORTH WEST ENGLAND AND THE ISLE OF MAN

Cycling the Pennine Bridleway
Isle of Man Coastal Path
The Lancashire Cycleway
The Lune Valley and Howgills
Walking in Cumbria's Eden Valley
Walking in Lancashire
Walking in the Forest of Bowland
  and Pendle

Walking on the Isle of Man
Walking on the West Pennine Moors
Walks in Silverdale and Arnside

LAKE DISTRICT

Cycling in the Lake District
Great Mountain Days in the
  Lake District
Joss Naylor's Lakes, Meres and
  Waters of the Lake District
Lake District Winter Climbs
Lake District: High Level and
  Fell Walks
Lake District: Low Level and
  Lake Walks
Mountain Biking in the Lake District
Outdoor Adventures with Children –
  Lake District
Scrambles in the Lake District –
  North
Scrambles in the Lake District –
  South
The Cumbria Way
Trail and Fell Running in the
  Lake District
Walking the Lake District Fells –
  Borrowdale
  Buttermere
  Coniston
  Keswick
  Langdale
  Mardale and the Far East
  Patterdale
  Wasdale
Walking the Tour of the Lake District

DERBYSHIRE, PEAK DISTRICT AND MIDLANDS

Cycling in the Peak District
Dark Peak Walks
Scrambles in the Dark Peak
Walking in Derbyshire
Walking in the Peak District –
  White Peak East
Walking in the Peak District –
  White Peak West

SOUTHERN ENGLAND

20 Classic Sportive Rides in
  South East England
20 Classic Sportive Rides in
  South West England
Cycling in the Cotswolds
Mountain Biking on the
  North Downs
Mountain Biking on the
  South Downs
Walking the South West Coast Path
South West Coast Path Map Booklets
  Vol 1: Minehead to St Ives
  Vol 2: St Ives to Plymouth
  Vol 3: Plymouth to Poole

Shorter Walks in the Dolomites
Ski Touring and Snowshoeing in
   the Dolomites
The Way of St Francis
Trekking in the Apennines
Trekking in the Dolomites
Trekking the Giants' Trail: Alta Via 1
   through the Italian Pennine Alps
Via Ferratas of the Italian Dolomites
   Vols 1&2
Walking and Trekking in the
   Gran Paradiso
Walking in Abruzzo
Walking in Italy's Cinque Terre
Walking in Italy's Stelvio
   National Park
Walking in Sicily
Walking in the Dolomites
Walking in Tuscany
Walking in Umbria
Walking Lake Como and Maggiore
Walking Lake Garda and Iseo
Walking on the Amalfi Coast
Walking the Via Francigena
   pilgrim route – Parts 2&3
Walks and Treks in the
   Maritime Alps

MEDITERRANEAN

The High Mountains of Crete
Trekking in Greece
Treks and Climbs in Wadi Rum,
   Jordan
Walking and Trekking in Zagori
Walking and Trekking on Corfu
Walking in Cyprus
Walking on Malta
Walking on the Greek Islands –
   the Cyclades

NEW ZEALAND
AND AUSTRALIA

Hiking the Overland Track

NORTH AMERICA

The John Muir Trail
The Pacific Crest Trail

SOUTH AMERICA

Aconcagua and the Southern Andes
Hiking and Biking Peru's Inca Trails
Torres del Paine

SCANDINAVIA, ICELAND
AND GREENLAND

Hiking in Norway – South
Trekking in Greenland – The Arctic
   Circle Trail
Trekking the Kungsleden
Walking and Trekking in Iceland

SLOVENIA, CROATIA,
MONTENEGRO AND ALBANIA

Mountain Biking in Slovenia
The Islands of Croatia
The Julian Alps of Slovenia
The Mountains of Montenegro
The Peaks of the Balkans Trail
The Slovene Mountain Trail
Walking in Slovenia: The Karavanke
Walks and Treks in Croatia

SPAIN AND PORTUGAL

Camino de Santiago:
   Camino Frances
Coastal Walks in Andalucia
Cycling the Camino de Santiago
Cycling the Ruta Via de la Plata
Mountain Walking in Mallorca
Mountain Walking in
   Southern Catalunya
Portugal's Rota Vicentina
Spain's Sendero Historico: The GR1
The Andalucian Coast to Coast Walk
The Camino del Norte and
   Camino Primitivo
The Camino Ingles and Ruta do Mar
The Camino Portugues
The Mountains of Nerja
The Mountains of Ronda
   and Grazalema
The Sierras of Extremadura
Trekking in Mallorca
Trekking in the Canary Islands
Trekking the GR7 in Andalucia
Walking and Trekking in the
   Sierra Nevada
Walking in Andalucia
Walking in Menorca
Walking in Portugal
Walking in the Algarve
Walking on the Azores
Walking in the Cordillera Cantabrica
Walking on Gran Canaria
Walking on La Gomera and El Hierro
Walking on La Palma
Walking on Lanzarote
   and Fuerteventura
Walking on Madeira
Walking on Tenerife
Walking on the Costa Blanca
Walking the Camino dos Faros

SWITZERLAND

Switzerland's Jura Crest Trail
The Swiss Alpine Pass Route –
   Via Alpina Route 1
The Swiss Alps
Tour of the Jungfrau Region
Walking in the Bernese Oberland

Walking in the Engadine –
   Switzerland
Walking in the Valais
Walking in Zermatt and Saas-Fee

JAPAN AND ASIA

Hiking and Trekking in the Japan
   Alps and Mount Fuji
Japan's Kumano Kodo Pilgrimage
Trekking in Tajikistan

HIMALAYA

Annapurna
Everest: A Trekker's Guide
Trekking in the Himalaya
Trekking in Bhutan
Trekking in Ladakh

MOUNTAIN LITERATURE

8000 metres
A Walk in the Clouds
Abode of the Gods
Fifty Years of Adventure
The Pennine Way – the Path,
   the People, the Journey
Unjustifiable Risk?

TECHNIQUES

Fastpacking
Geocaching in the UK
Map and Compass
Outdoor Photography
Polar Exploration
The Mountain Hut Book

MINI GUIDES

Alpine Flowers
Navigation
Pocket First Aid and
   Wilderness Medicine
Snow

For full information on all our guides,
books and eBooks,
visit our website:
www.cicerone.co.uk

CICERONE

Trust Cicerone to guide your next adventure, wherever it may be around the world...

Discover guides for hiking, mountain walking, backpacking, trekking, trail running, cycling and mountain biking, ski touring, climbing and scrambling in Britain, Europe and worldwide.

Connect with Cicerone online and find inspiration.

- buy books and ebooks
- articles, advice and trip reports
- podcasts and live events
- GPX files and updates
- regular newsletter

cicerone.co.uk